MW00584026

THE 5 TRUTHS FOR TRANSFORMATIONAL LEADERS

ED MISHRELL

THE 5 TRUTHS FOR

TRANSFORMATIONAL

LEADERS

HOW NONPROFIT ORGANIZATIONS THRIVE, GROW, AND MAKE A PROFOUND DIFFERENCE

WILEY

Published by John Wiley & Sons, Inc., Hoboken, New Jersey.
Published simultaneously in Canada.

For general information on our other products and services or for technical support, please contact our Customer Care Department within the United States at (800) 762-2974, outside the United States at (317) 572-3993 or fax (317) 572-4002.

Wiley also publishes its books in a variety of electronic formats. Some content that appears in print may not be available in electronic formats. For more information about Wiley products, visit our web site at www.wiley.com.

Library of Congress Cataloging-in-Publication Data:

Names: Mishrell, Ed, author.
Title: The 5 truths for transformational leaders: how nonprofit organizations thrive, grow, and make a profound difference / Ed Mishrell.
Other titles: Five truths for transformational leaders
Description: First edition. | Hoboken, New Jersey: Wiley, [2023] | Includes bibliographical references and index.
Identifiers: LCCN 2022056913 (print) | LCCN 2022056914 (ebook) | ISBN 9781394187003 (hardback) | ISBN 9781394187027 (adobe pdf) | ISBN 9781394187010 (epub)
Subjects: LCSH: Nonprofit organizations—Management. | Leadership.
Classification: LCC HD62.6 .M57 2023 (print) | LCC HD62.6 (ebook) | DDC 361.7/63—dc23/eng/20221202
LC record available at https://lccn.loc.gov/2022056913
LC ebook record available at https://lccn.loc.gov/2022056914

Cover Design: Wiley
Cover Image: © malerapaso/Getty Images

This book is dedicated to the millions of people who lead and support the missions of nonprofit organizations.

Contents

Acknowledgments

Thank you to my beautiful spouse, partner, and best friend, Leslie Mishrell. Your support and encouragement made me believe I could do this.

I would like to thank and acknowledge the transformational board and professional leaders I had the privilege of interviewing. I greatly admire your wisdom, your dedication, your belief in your mission, and the amazing difference you make every day. I hope I have successfully captured how you achieved incredible results. Thank you Howard Architzel, Rebecca Asmo, Corky Bowerman, Kimberly Boyd, Kaye Brewer, Tommy Breymeier, Suzie Glaze Burt, Shirley Carraway, Carter Clark, Greg Cushing, Julie Daniels, Tony Dickinson, Patrick Doyle, Heather Ehle, Michael Frazier, Amelia Gibson, Donyell Jones, Nicholas Jones, Reece Kurtenbach, Bridgett Laird, Vanessa Merhib, Misty L. Miller, Tara Lynn Mills, David Morley, Larry and Diane Ness, Timothy Pate, Robyn Peery, Jason Reuter, Judith Ranger Smith, Jodie Warth, and James Pierce.

There are a number of people I asked for advice and wisdom when I began researching the book and for feedback on drafts of the book. It is a privilege to be your friend and colleague. Thank you for your advice, wisdom, encouragement, and support Jeff Amy, Jeff Benatti, Jim Caufield, Kirk Dominick, Donna Ferraro, Elizabeth Fowlkes, Pam Hodges, Ronnie Jenkins, George Krupanski, Kim Madrigal, Fred Miller, Lorraine Orr, Glenn Permuy, and Debbie Verges. Thank you, Jim Clark, for your advice an encouragement: you were part of this project from beginning to end.

Thank you to the national nonprofit leaders and leaders of organizations who support leadership development for your thoughts, wisdom, insights, and leadership:

Jennifer Blatz, president and CEO, StriveTogether
Owen Charter, president and CEO, Boy & Girls Clubs of Canada

Jim Clark, president and CEO, Boys & Girls Clubs of America
Patrick Cisler, president and CEO, Lakeshore Nonprofits
Kirk Dominick, president and CEO, World Federation of Youth Clubs
Charlotte Haberaecker, president and CEO, Lutheran Services in America
Commissioner Kenneth Hodder, national commander, The Salvation Army
Undraye Howard, senior vice president, diversity, equity and inclusion,
    Social Current
Stephanie Hull, president and CEO, Girls Inc.
Jody Levison-Johnson, president and CEO, Social Current
Suzanne McCormick, president and CEO, YMCA of the USA
Jonathan Reckford, CEO, Habitat for Humanity International
Jennifer Sirangelo, president and CEO, National 4 H Council
Artis Stevens, president and CEO, Big Brothers Big Sisters of America
Schroeder Stribling, president and CEO, Mental Health America
Wendy Thomas, president and CEO, Leadership Tulsa

Thank you to my literary agent, Marisa Cleveland. I appreciate your enthusiasm, energy, and encouragement. I knew from the first time we spoke that you were the perfect literary agent for me.

Thank you, Brian Neill, editor at Wiley, for believing in the book and bringing it into the world.

Thank you to copyeditor Susan Geraghty for making the book readable and well organized.

A special thank you to my great friend, Evan McElroy. You not only encouraged me but you also read every draft and provided excellent feedback.

Foreword

It's no secret that the key ingredient to the success of any organization, large or small, is leadership. The right leader is a game changer in every aspect. They surround themselves with people who excel in advancing the vision, mission, and performance of the organization. They form strong relationships, focus the organization on key outcomes, and drive the business to deliver results. The right leader makes *all* the difference! That's why I'm so excited about the publication of *The 5 Truths for Transformational Leaders*. It provides a leadership model to strengthen the impact of nonprofit organizations, because leading a nonprofit is different.

The author, Ed Mishrell, has extensive experience in the nonprofit industry, serving at every level from student intern to a senior leader at Boys & Girls Clubs of America (BGCA). Throughout his career he has seen virtually every type of leader, enabling him to understand the key levers that drive a successful nonprofit enterprise. This enabled Ed to successfully lead numerous national initiatives for BGCA, many of which focused on leadership development. One of his crowning achievements was BGCA's Advanced Leadership Program—a program that unleashes the best in leaders and puts them to work with their team in a dynamic environment. I participated in this program's inaugural cohort while serving as the CEO of Boys & Girls Clubs of Greater Milwaukee. It honed my skills as a leader and helped my leadership team focus on our most important priorities, which laid the foundation for an incredible growth trajectory and deeper community impact. When I took on the leadership of BGCA, I had the privilege of working directly with Ed. I had a front row seat to observe how Ed's own leadership competencies shaped numerous advancements for the BGCA mission and enterprise. He is a master collaborator, coach, and thought partner. He has the unique ability to bring strategy to action and cast an inspiring vision that others want to follow.

There are numerous books on leadership, but few focused on nonprofit organizations. This book is significant because it provides a mission-driven leadership model. As the title states, the book is about *transformation*, in contrast to incremental advances in performance, scale, or impact. It brings together real-life examples of organizations that have made transformational advances with time-tested leadership attributes that enable success. This book is a breakthrough set of lessons in what it takes to be a nonprofit leader, making it a major contribution to the nonprofit profession and sector.

As Vince Lombardi famously said, "Leaders aren't born, they are made." *The 5 Truths for Transformational Leaders* is the practical, step-by-step guide to build your personal leadership playbook to advance your mission. Whether you currently lead a nonprofit or aspire to one day, your capacity as a leader will be enhanced by the lessons in this book. One significant aspect of the book is that each chapter contains a special section for board members on their leadership role and how they can support leadership development of professional staff members. The book also provides guidance for board members on making the most important choice any board must make: hiring the right leader!

Whether you are a board volunteer or a professional leader, the lessons in this book will help you deepen your mission impact. Philanthropists, civic leaders, and government officials will also benefit by better understanding the elements needed to strengthen nonprofit organizations and help them achieve results.

My favorite of *The 5 Truths* is the first one: be fanatical about the mission. If your mission matters, then it matters how it is led. We need bold, transformational leaders in the nonprofit sector. I have a strong belief in the American dream and American promise. Fulfilling on these foundational virtues of our country can and will happen only through transformational leadership. The stronger leaders we become, the stronger our nation will be in the future.

Let's get started.

Jim Clark
President and CEO, Boys & Girls Clubs of America

THE 5 TRUTHS FOR TRANSFORMATIONAL LEADERS

Introduction
The Origin of the Five Truths for Transformational Leaders

"Change in transformational leadership is special, deep and broad."
James M. Burns

According to a report by the Urban Institute entitled "The Nonprofit Sector in Brief 2020," there are 1.5 million nonprofit organizations in the United States. Nonprofit organizations have a strong belief in the promise of America. At their very core the missions and visions of nonprofit organizations are about supporting our aspirations as nation. Their collective missions are aligned with the beliefs put forth by our nation's founders: that all women and men are created equal and everyone has the right to life, liberty, and the pursuit of happiness. Nonprofits labor tirelessly to make every community a great place to live, work, play, learn, and raise a family. Their overarching goal is equity of opportunity for every woman, man, and child no matter their circumstances, where they live, where they were born, their race, their beliefs, their age, their sexual orientation, or their gender.

Some of these organizations struggle while others thrive and grow and make an incredible difference. Many experience a continuous boom-and-bust cycle—a good year followed by a year of struggle. Although many factors determine success, I believe leadership is the preeminent factor in determining how successful a nonprofit organization will be in achieving its mission. "Leadership capacity of nonprofit and voluntary organizations will definitely determine whether or not the basic goals and ambitions of these organizations are effectively accomplished" (Seyhan, 2013, p. 256). There are thousands of books about leadership but most of what is written is based on the experiences of business and government. I believe leading a nonprofit is different, and it is more difficult. Nonprofits operate in a complex environment with multiple stakeholders and ever-changing conditions. Measuring success is difficult, and authority to make decisions is shared. These organizations require exceptional leadership to thrive. The goal of this book is to provide a leadership model that enables nonprofit leaders to achieve profound impact on the lives of millions of people.

Warren Bennis observed that "excellence is a better teacher than mediocrity. The lessons of the ordinary are everywhere. Truly profound and original insights are to be found only in studying the exemplary" (Bennis and Biederman, 1997, p. 8). Based on that belief, I concluded the best way to learn about transformational leadership was to benchmark board and staff leaders of organizations who experienced a transformation. The challenge was how to identify the exemplary. There is not a universal measurement for nonprofit success. I first spoke with some of the incredible leaders I had the privilege of working with throughout my career. These conversations provided a starting point.

I then identified organizations that achieved increases in their operating budget of 100% or more over a five-year period as compared with the 4% average increase of revenue across the sector (Urban Institute, 2020). The organizations studied all started with budgets under $2 million when the CEO who drove transformation was hired. All of them more than doubled their operating budget in five years. Some tripled and quadrupled their budgets. I then looked at other organizational data to determine if the increase in funding also led to increased reach and impact.

I interviewed chief professional officers (CPOs), staff members, and board leaders from these organizations. I interviewed the CPOs first, followed by the board leaders, other staff, and in some cases donors who played a significant role in the organization's transformation. The goal of the interviews was to identify and describe what these leaders did that made a difference and the role others played.

The organizations I studied generally fell into one of three groups when the CEO who led the transformation was hired:

- The organization was struggling. In some instances, these were organizations that had thrived at one time, but had been in a period of decline. Some had experienced significant turnover in leadership.
- The organization had been doing okay. They were neither growing nor declining.

- The organization had a significant opportunity to grow that required significant change and the capacity for acting quickly.

This book represents what I learned. It provides a mission-driven leadership model to inspire and guide board members, professionals, volunteers, and investors to drive increased impact and reach. It provides a model for building organizations that strengthen communities and make a significant and lasting difference in the lives of millions of people. For nonprofits this means becoming bigger, more capable, more impactful, and more essential to building strong communities. Successful organizations gain momentum and are able to attract resources and people who want to make a difference.

From the interviews, observations, and my own experience, I found that what makes a transformational leader comes down to five truths that apply to professional and board leaders. Boards are integral to the organization's success. Every chapter ends with notes for board members. Transformation is only possible if the board and staff work together as partners.

I believe the five truths for transformational leaders apply to all leaders regardless of size or the focus of their mission. In many ways there are no secrets to transformational leadership. None of the five truths is surprising. What transformational leaders do best is stay ultra-focused on mission and execute on basic organizational development principles very, very, very well. These leaders are driven, disciplined, humble, and transparent.

Following is a summary of the five truths of transformational leadership:

Truth 1: Be Fanatical About Mission. Nonprofits are founded on and driven by mission. Interviews with leaders and board members who achieved unprecedented growth suggest a deep belief in and commitment to the mission is the most important characteristic of a transformational leader. Fanatical about mission means mission drives every decision, every conversation, and every hire. Hiring a leader with a fanatic belief and commitment to mission and the capacity to lead is a priority. Strong, unwavering identification with mission is not enough by itself, but without it the rest does not matter. You can't fake mission. A fanatic belief in mission empowers leaders to inspire others, make difficult decisions and set high standards for services that deliver life-changing results.

Truth 2: **Fix, Stabilize, or Replace Systems, Practices, and People Who Are Not Working.** Only incremental improvement is possible until the organization stabilizes day-to-day operations. It is difficult to grow when every day brings a new crisis and problems to solve that could be avoided. There are two critical tasks for transformational leaders:

- **Establish practices, process, and policies to achieve maximum efficiency.** Before an organization can grow and transform it must stabilize day-to-day operations by establishing systems, process, and standard practices that are universally applied across the organization. These are the basic ingredients for well-managed organizations that operate efficiently. It is difficult to grow when leaders spend most of the day solving problems.
- **Make needed staff changes.** Fixing and replacing what is not working also applies to people. Transformation requires dedicated and talented staff fully committed and prepared to carry out the organization's mission. Making tough decisions about people is the most difficult part of being a leader. Even when the grievances are severe it can be difficult to act. Focus on mission gives leaders the will to make difficult decisions.

Truth 3: **Establish a Mission-Driven Strategy.** The leader must develop, articulate, and align the organization on a well-thought-out strategy for how the organization will succeed, thrive, and achieve its mission. Leaders must answer four questions and weave them into a compelling story that inspires, aligns, and energizes.

- To achieve our mission, who will we serve and what difference will we make?
- What services will we provide to achieve our outcomes and how will we know we are succeeding?
- How will we build an organization with the capability and the talent to achieve these outcomes?
- How will we acquire the resources we need to succeed?

Truth 4: Execution Drives Results: Execution requires clarity and universal understanding about the organization's strategy and the discipline to stay focused on what will make the biggest difference. There are always many good ideas; leaders must clearly identify and stay focused on what is most important. This is only possible if the priorities are clear and measurable. Success is characterized by achieving the following:

- Relentlessly communicating the strategy at every opportunity over and over and over again
- Staying focused on what is most important
- Establishing an annual plan with clear priorities, targets, and progress measures
- Executing the plan

Truth 5: Continue to Grow as a Leader. Evolving and continuing to grow as a leader can be a challenge. Some leaders can lead an initial transformation. They are able to stabilize and build efficient operating mechanisms and attract a strong team, but then they become stuck. Instead of continuing to evolve as the leadership needs of the organization change, they work harder at doing what worked initially. Transformational leaders are able to adapt and change their focus to meet the evolving needs of a growing organization. These successful leaders make sure to do the following:

- **Adopt a growth mindset.** People with a growth mindset believe they have the capacity to grow and develop new skills. They take steps every day to support that belief and nurture their personal growth.
- **Continuously seek feedback.** Feedback from those who know us best is the key to identifying blind spots, behaviors that are holding us back, and skill sets we need to improve or acquire.
- **Recognize and act on what the organization needs now and in the future.** Transformational leaders continuously scan the organization and the external environment to identify challenges, issues, and trends that could affect their organization.

The final chapter, "The Road Ahead: Trends and Challenges That Will Shape the Future," explores emerging trends and challenges that will shape the future for nonprofit organizations and how the nonprofit sector prepares leaders to meet these challenges. This chapter is based on conversations with the leaders of large national networks and include these topics:

- **Workforce challenges:** Organizations big and small are competing to hire and retain talented people. Nonprofits have difficulty competing financially, and in many instances the work is mentally and emotionally challenging. Successful leaders must be at the forefront of defining the future of work to attract talented, dedicated people.

- **Measuring and achieving outcomes.** Funders want to be able to show the resources they provide make a difference. Savvy leaders understand that making decisions based on data not only aids fundraising but also enables continuous learning about how to increase impact. Successful leaders will continue to advance and build measurement into everything the organization does.

- **Creation of partnerships, collaborations, and collective impact networks.** With limited resources the need to work together as one network that makes a difference for the community is greater than ever. Leaders who thrive in this environment must be collaborative, innovative, and committed to a collective community mission that supersedes their organization. Business, government, philanthropists, and nonprofits must work together to establish a plan for coordinating services across the entire community.

Chapter Organization

Each chapter provides a full explanation of one of the five truths. Each truth is supported by observations from staff members, board members, and CPOs of organizations that achieved transformational growth. In addition to the explanation of each of the five truths for transformational leaders each chapter contains three other sections:

- **The story of the Community Centers of Mission City.** Throughout the book, you'll find the story of the five truths as told through the experience of a fictional organization—the Community Centers of Mission City—which reflect many of the challenges, struggles, and breakthroughs transformational leaders must face. Their story begins in the first chapter with the board divided about selecting a new CPO who can revitalize the organization. Their choice may surprise you. At the end of this introduction you'll find background information on the Community Centers of Mission City.

- **Notes for board members.** The board members I interviewed provided incredible wisdom and insight. Many of their comments are used throughout the manuscript, but at the end of every chapter there is a special section that explores the critical role board members play in organizational transformation. In fact, organizational transformation and growth can occur only when the right staff leader and the right board leadership are working together. When asked to give advice to other nonprofit boards about how they can drive unprecedented growth and make a bigger difference in their community many board leaders suggested it started with the board answering two questions: Do we have the right leader? And do we have the right board?

- **Resource Center.** Each chapter contains a list of tools and resources available to support staff and board members in adopting each of the five truths. The resources are listed at the end of each chapter with a full version of each resource at the back of the book. The resources will also be available on a Five Truths webpage (p.175).

Background Information
The Community Centers of Mission City

Mission Statement

Work collaboratively to provide children and families in underserved communities with access to programs and resources to empower them to thrive.

Vision

Every neighborhood in Mission City is a great place to live, work, play, and raise a family.

The Community Centers of Mission City was founded in 1964. The founding board included some of Mission City's most prominent citizens. For many years, the organization was one of the city's leading nonprofit organizations. Many of Mission City's most successful citizens benefited from the programs and services. They testify that it changed the course of their lives. As the founding board aged, the organization struggled to find new board leadership. Financial support declined. There have been five CEOs in the past decade.

- *Mission City population: 450,000*
- *Current budget: $912,000*
- *Two facilities*
- ***Programs:*** *After-school childcare, senior citizen center, teen center, food distribution, and adult education. In addition, the community centers served as a meeting place for many community groups and other nonprofits. For example, after-school childcare is provided by the Boys & Girls Clubs and a local hospital operates a clinic four days a week. The Mission City Community Centers have always worked to bring services to the community to make them easy to access.*
- ***Funding:*** *United Way of Greater Mission City, Mission County Children's Services, an annual gala, program fees primarily for summer program and a small endowment that is shrinking. The organization has committed to conducting its first comprehensive annual campaign.*
- ***Staffing:*** *CPO, resource development director, two center directors, 2 program directors, 1 administrative assistance/bookkeeper, and 14 part-time staff members.*
- ***Board:*** *15 board members: 8 with 20-plus years of service, 2 with 5 years of service, and 5 with less than 2 years of service.*

1

Truth 1:
Be Fanatical
About Mission

"What matters is not the leader's charisma. What matters is the leader's mission."

Peter F. Drucker, *Managing the Non-Profit Organization*

Nonprofit organizations are created by people coming together around a mission to make their community a better place to live, work, play, and raise a family. Their mission is the reason for existence. The book *Joan Garry's Guide to Nonprofit Leadership* summarizes the importance of mission: "Your mission statement is your North Star. The big thing that matters most" (Garry, 2017, p. 22). Although this seems obvious, the best leaders—the ones that transform their organization—are manically and fanatically driven by mission. They lead with mission, make every decision to further the mission, aim every resource at achieving the mission, and inspire others to support the mission. This is the first and most important truth for transformational leaders. It is not sufficient by itself but being fanatical about mission is the foundation for the other four truths. A leader with an unwavering fanatical commitment to mission inspires others, raises expectations, and is able to make difficult decisions about people, strategy, and the allocation of resources.

Let's begin by attending a very important meeting of the Community Centers of Mission City board of directors.

Community Centers of Mission City
Board Meeting Summary

The meeting of the board of directors of the Community Centers of Mission City began at 12:00 noon. The agenda called for the board to make the most important decision boards ever make: hiring a CPO. Joan Fenz is the chairperson of the search committee. Joan joined the board 18 months ago. She is a living example of the organization's mission and impact. Joan attributes her success to the guidance and encouragement she received at the Southside Community Center when she was a child. She believes in the organization's mission and understands the community needs a strong organization capable of making a difference for young people and families.

Joan quickly became frustrated with the board. The organization was stuck, constantly struggling to find the resources they needed. Every few months there was a financial crisis followed by intense activity to "keep the doors open." Somehow, they found the resources to continue but soon found themselves back in the same position. Staff turnover was an issue and many of the staff members who stayed were not the superstars the organization's mission demanded.

Joan pushed the board to make a leadership change. The organization churned through five different CPOs in the past 10 years. She believed they needed a leader with the drive to pull the organization together, make a difference in the community, and reestablish the organization's credibility. She believed the most important talent needed by their leader was the ability to excite others about the mission and the difference the Community Centers make.

The board finally resolved that the organization must improve. After much debate, the board asked their CPO to resign. The board chair, Hank Salvan, had recently retired and agreed to become the interim CPO. The board formed a search committee led by Joan to find a transformational leader. The search committee resolved to hire a leader who was up to the challenge. They designed a thorough process to identify candidates and select someone who could transform the organization. They received more than 50 applications, *many with experience as a CPO at similar-sized organizations. There was one internal applicant. A review of résumés identified five candidates who were interviewed by the search committee. The search committee narrowed the field to two finalists.*

One finalist, Harold, was a seasoned CPO with 10 years of experience in resource development and 4 years as the CPO of a similar-sized nonprofit focused on environmental issues in a neighboring community. He had the experience the board had outlined in the job description. Under his leadership the organization he led had averaged 5% annual growth in income.

The other finalist was the internal candidate, Helen. Helen did not have experience as a CPO and almost no experience in finance, HR, board development, or program management. She had worked for Mission City University in resource development for four years and had been the director of resource development for the Community Centers of Mission City for 14 months. Helen had been a great support to Hank during his time as interim CPO. During the past four months she had been indispensable to the survival of the organization. She had taken on extra tasks and proved to be a quick learner. She demonstrated a deep passion and commitment to the Center's mission. Her enthusiasm was contagious.

Every board member was invited to meet the two finalists as part of a final interview. All 10 board members present today had met and interviewed both final candidates.

As the meeting began Joan handed out a copy of the résumé of each candidate and a list of pros and cons for each prepared by the search committee. The differences were clear. Harold had experience in the competencies the board had prioritized in the job description (fund raising, board development, financial management, and planning) but little experience with a community-based organization. The organization he led was primarily focused on educating the public about environmental issues. Helen had an abundance of energy and passion for their mission but little experience beyond resource development. In fact, her only supervisory experience was supervising a student intern.

The four members of the search committee were split on whom to hire. Two felt Harold, the person with proven experience, was what the organization needed. This half believed they needed someone who knows how to lead the organization out of crisis and reach a point of stability. They recognized the person would need to embrace their mission and learn about the communities they served but believed that was not insurmountable. Board members could introduce them to key leaders in the community. Harold had expressed a strong interest in the mission during the interview and asked many questions about the programs the Center offered.

The other two members of the committee felt they needed someone who believed deeply in the cause, someone who could excite staff, donors, and the community. Although experience was important, they put a higher priority on hiring someone who could lead the organization forward. They recognized Helen did not have the experience or skill sets laid out in the job description, but she had a spark that excited them. The board members who wanted to hire Helen, which included Joan, pointed out that the last three CPOs had experience but were not viewed as a leader by the staff or the community. "I believe Helen is a leader; she can excite people about our mission. In two years, she will transform this organization," Joan told the board.

During the interview process Helen was clear about her lack of experience; in fact, she followed up her initial interview by sending the board a detailed plan for her first 100 days as CPO. The plan addressed what she had already learned working with Hank and how she would learn to successfully manage all aspects of the ongoing operations of the organization. The plan also included a goal to increase operating revenue by 20% in her first year.

The entire board agreed this was a plus for her.

After nearly an hour of intense discussion, the board was still unable to decide. Half wanted Harold, the proven executive, and half wanted Helen. Joan suggested they table the discussion and that

Hank and the search committee would check both candidate's references and interview each candidate again to address the areas about each candidate the board was concerned about. They would come back to the board with a recommendation. She said, "Maybe we need to think about this differently than we have in the past. We need to determine what we absolutely need from our CPO and figure out how we support everything else."

What does a different way of thinking look like? In October 1997 Billy Beane became the general manager of the Oakland Athletics baseball team. The year before, the new owners of the team slashed payroll after having the highest payroll in the American League. The challenge for Beane was to field a team with a modest budget that could compete with the Yankees and other big-market teams that had large budgets for player salaries. To succeed, Beane realized he had to look at players through a different lens. Beane used sabermetrics to build teams on a small budget that won their division championship between 2000 and 2003 and set a record for the longest regular season winning streak. His approach changed how every Major League Baseball team evaluated talent.

Board members of many social service organizations, especially those with smaller budgets, have a similar challenge. To succeed and grow, organizations must compete head-to-head for resources (money, talent, customers) with organizations with similar missions, larger budgets, and specialized expertise. Larger organizations typically have an experienced leader and a team of experts to lead resource development, finance, operations, HR, and other major areas of the organization. Their size also gives them visibility, legitimacy, and access—a seat at the table with community leaders.

The leader of smaller organizations must oversee all these functions personally, lead the organization, and manage service delivery. But financially you can't afford to hire a CPO with multiple years of proven resource development success, outstanding communication skills, board savvy, financial management, and documented success as a leader driven by a passion for mission. The CPO you want to hire is likely not available to you. So, what is your strategy for hiring a CPO with the capacity to transform your organization?

Hiring the most experienced leader you can find may not be the best answer. Like Billy Beane and the Oakland As, to be successful and compete with larger organizations, you may need to look at filling this position through a different lens.

Interviews with leaders who have achieved unprecedented growth suggest that hiring someone with a deep passionate commitment to mission and the capacity to lead is the most important characteristics you need to hire. In many cases the leaders who transformed organizations did not start with the skills or experience boards typically prioritize. Yet these organizations grew their operating budgets and income at more than five times the average over an extended period of time. Every organization I benchmarked more than doubled their operating budget between 2012 and 2018, with some tripling and even quadrupling their operating budget.

Transformational leaders—staff and board members—recognize that transformation begins with a fanatic belief in the importance of the mission. Although everyone working for a nonprofit believes in the mission, some leaders embody the mission in a deep and profound way that sets them apart. For these leaders, every decision, every thought, every action is focused on furthering the mission. Here is a summary of how board members described the importance of belief in mission in their CPO's success:

She cares deeply about the mission. It is always front of mind. Every decision is based on how the organization can better achieve mission.

The core of her being is focused on helping others.

You could see his passion for kids right away. He had a combination of enthusiasm, passion, and knowledge about what to do.

He had little experience with board, fund raising, and finance compared to other candidates, but he had something others did not: a deep passion for the mission.

She has a great passion for the Club, she excited everyone she spoke to about what the Club could accomplish.

It is hard to articulate until you meet the right person. The reasons we hired him are not generally in the job description. In the end the board determined we needed a mission-driven, big-picture thinker.

Her passion was uplifting. We could imagine her exciting others to support the organization.

The leader must believe deeply in the mission and be willing to work tire-lessly to make the organization successful.

One of the organizations interviewed for this book was in the process of replacing an extremely successful CPO when I was conducting interviews. Under her leadership the organization's operating budget of nearly $300,000 rose to an operating budget of over $3 million in 2018. The board had set up a comprehensive hiring process, interviewed several candidates, and narrowed it down to two finalists they invited for a second interview. In the end the board decided that neither was the right candidate. They chose to start the process over again. What happened? The board determined they needed someone with the *passion* their previous CPO brought every day and who could manage the big picture.

The successful CPOs I interviewed identified their passion, commitment, and belief in the organization's mission as one of their greatest strengths as a leader. Mission was the reason they wanted to be a leader and it was what drove every decision, every action, and every conversation.

I love the mission. I believe deeply in it; everyone sees how I feel.
My mindset is always focused on the mission.
If I stay true to my core values, I can accomplish what we need to. Most important is always being true to our mission.
I am always mission focused and focused on our kids. Constantly asking, are they safe? Are we making a difference? How can we get better?
I am always mission driven.
If I am focused on mission, I can make the tough calls. I have no secret talent that makes me successful. My skill is I will work hard and my belief and focus on mission.

When staff members were asked what the CPO's three greatest strengths were, nearly everyone named belief and commitment to mission first. Here are some examples of what they said:

She is genuine and has a deep belief in mission. Always mission driven.
   Amazed staff, board, and key stakeholders about what he thought the Club could be for members. He had extremely high expectations.

He believed our members need a safe place, love, and structure—he will never abandon his beliefs.

She never compromises when it comes to mission and values.

She is genuine and has a deep belief in mission. Always mission driven.

Absolute commitment to the mission. The board gets our mission, but he puts mission at the heart of every discussion and every decision.

She cares deeply about the mission. It is always front of mind. Every decision is made based on how the organization can better achieve mission.

Three Reasons for a Fanatical Believe in Mission

The views of board and professional leaders about the importance of mission suggest three very important reasons why a deep belief in the mission is critical to success:

First, passion is contagious. It inspires and attracts other people passionate about your mission. The leader's deeply held belief brings out the best in other people. Most of us long to be engaged in something bigger than ourselves. We may be guarded about displaying our passion until we find others with the same deep beliefs. Someone who exemplifies dedication to an important cause; someone who aspires to make our communities better places to live, work, play, and raise our families; inspires everyone around them to make a difference. Of course, effective leaders must do more than believe in mission, but the rest does not matter if they are not able to exude excitement and passion about the importance of the organization's mission and vision from every part of their being.

One staff person shared that one of the CPO's greatest strengths was the "ability to communicate the mission and vision in a manner that excites potential donors and collaborators. People want to be part of something that is moving forward." Another board member shared she was not on the board when they were selecting the CPO, but as an important community leader, the board asked her to meet with the final candidate and let them know if she believed he was the right person for the job. She was extremely impressed by the person's passion. She not only recommended that the board hire him but also she subsequently asked if she could join the board.

Of course, to be credible, the leader must also be able to articulate the outcomes the organization will achieve and how the organization will achieve them. In Chapter 3 we will explore how leaders develop and communicate a strategy for how organizations make a difference and achieve its mission.

Second, belief in mission empowers leaders with the fortitude to make tough calls. Every leader must make difficult calls about people, strategy, and allocation of scarce resources. Too often the status quo prevails. The lack of momentum in the "we always did it this way" attitude defeats opportunities for transformation. In the end decisions must be based on mission. A fanatic commitment to mission gives leaders the edge needed to make difficult calls.

Transformation begins with a constituency of one—one leader willing and able to see the big picture and make choices to achieve a greater end. One board member noted that the CPO does not let anything or anyone get in the way of accomplishing our goals. Transformational leaders are able to make tough decisions and stand by them. Another board member noted that the CPO had to be willing to make a lot of tough decisions.

Nearly every organization studied for this book had to make changes early in their tenure about staff. These are never easy, no matter the circumstances. No one wants to tell someone they no longer have a job. Passion for mission empowers leaders to see the bigger picture and take actions needed for the organization to move on. People invest in organizations and leaders they believe will use their resources effectively. Fanatic commitment to mission tells people the leader will deploy their resources for maximum impact.

One leader noted that it is painful to watch people they care about not grow with the organization. But if their skill set is no longer what the organization needs, leaders must make a change. It is hard to make these decisions. Focusing on mission supersedes all other actions. People provide resources to support our mission and the leader is responsible for making sure they are fully used. If staff members are not right for your mission a change is required.

Third, commitment to mission demands impeccably high standards of excellence that are never compromised. The expectations leaders have for themselves permeate the entire organization. They affect everyone—staff and board members, investors, community, and every stakeholder. The missions and goals of nonprofit organizations seek to make life richer, provide opportunities for challenged populations, and take care of people struggling with illness, physical challenges, or lack of resources. These missions deserve and demand excellence. Successful leaders never settle for good enough. They have high expectations for themselves and everyone around them. Mission-driven leaders push themselves and the entire organization to continuously improve. They have the discipline to keep mission in front of them when they make every decision—big and small. This means they often make the harder choice that pushes people out of their comfort zone.

Fanatical commitment to mission is not enough by itself, but without the commitment other traits and skills do not matter. (The Resource Center at the end of the book includes information to aid boards in hiring and onboarding a mission-driven CPO including a Board Member Guide to Hiring and Onboarding the CPO and a Fanatical About Mission Worksheet for aspiring leaders.) The leaders interviewed all demonstrated other traits. In many ways these are also supported by their commitment to mission.

- **Positive approach to problem-solving.** Transformational leaders always have a positive belief in the capacity of the organization to grow and create a greater future. They are continually focused on moving forward. They possess a growth mentality. They project an indomitable will to keep moving forward.
- **Transparent.** Transformational leaders are straight shooters; they have the courage to say what they believe. They are comfortable making themselves vulnerable. They constantly work to grow as a person and professional, never believing they are finished. One board member described their CPO as always open and approachable.
- **Intellectual curiosity and desire to learn.** Transformational leaders continuously search for ways to develop as a leader. They read about leadership, go to conferences, attend training, and benchmark other organizations and leaders. Every leader provided examples about how they applied something they learned to advance the organization.

Let's return to the board of the Community Centers of Mission City to see whom they decided to hire and what influenced their decision.

Questions and Thoughts for Aspiring

Community Centers of Mission City
Board Meeting One Month Later

Board chair Hank Salvan called the meeting to order. Thirteen of 15 board members were present and ready to determine who would be the next CPO. There was palpable energy in the room. Hank called the meeting to order and turned the meeting over to Joan Fenz, chair of the selection committee.

Joan began by outlining the steps the search committee had taken since the last meeting to learn more about their two final candidates. They checked references, conducted background checks, and informally interviewed each candidate over lunch. The candidates were provided a summary of where the board was in the hiring process.

Each candidate was asked four questions. The questions were shared with each candidate in advance:

- If hired what are your goals for your first month as CPO and how will you accomplish them?
- What part of the job do you feel will be most difficult for you? Why? How will you approach this challenge?
- What part of the job do you believe you are best prepared for? Why?
- How would you describe your belief in our mission? Tell us about a time you made an important decision based on the mission of the organization? What was the decision? How did mission affect your thinking? What was the outcome?

The background checks and references were positive for both candidates and generally supported what the board already knew. Harold had provided solid leadership to the organization he currently led. Helen was a superior performer at the college she worked for and was known for her positive spirit and commitment to the college. Board chair Salvan added that in the time he has served as interim

CPO Helen had taken on many extra assignments and performed at a high level. She was a quick learner and impressed everyone with her strong sense of purpose.

The interviews did reveal differences in how each would approach their initial time at the organization. Harold indicated he would focus more internally. He wanted to better understand the program at the Community Centers and the people they served in each community. He also recognized that on day one he needed to have a good knowledge of the organization's finances. He also planned to spend time with each board member to better understand how they viewed the organization's strengths and challenges.

Helen, who had submitted a first 100-day plan after her initial interview, outlined three goals:

Goal 1: Develop a positive relationship with key stakeholders. She said, "This is the most important goal. I want to meet with each board member, each of our donors, the staff, members of local advisory boards, and key community leaders. I want to find out how they view the organization, what their expectations of me are, and how we can get better. I will make a report to the board summarizing what I learn at the first board meeting."

Goal 2: Implement a plan to tighten up our daily routines. "Mr. Salvan has already started this process, we can gain efficiency and maintain better records by standardizing process."

Goal 3: Make safety a priority from her first day. "I will make this part of my interviews with staff. As we look to improve the quality of our services this is where we need to begin. Safety includes physical safety, but also making sure everyone entering our buildings is emotionally comfortable."

In conclusion Joan stated, "After considering everything the search committee is recommending that we hire Helen. This was not a unanimous decision; after much discussion, our vote was 3 to 1. We all recognized Helen's lack of experience, but we feel her passion for what we do is contagious. The energy she brings to everything sets her apart. I believe she will excite everyone involved with our organization.

"I do recognize that she does not have all the experience we out-lined in the job description. This board will need to provide her the support she needs to learn and grow. I believe that Helen is a leader with the potential to take our organization to new heights. Our last three CPOs all had experience but could not provide the leadership needed to advance the organization. We can't continue to hire experienced mediocracy and expect a different result."

A moment of silence followed Joan's remarks followed by a vigor-ous dialogue. Fredrick, who had been on the board for more than 25 years was the first to speak. "I agree we need a leader, not some-one who's strengths are managing day-to-day."

Jane, the chair of the board governance committee added, "I agree. I believe Helen has the potential to be a great leader. She is the right choice for us."

Albert, another long-time board member, disagreed. "We need stable leadership. I have not met either candidate, but Harold's résumé shows the proven experience we need. This Helen does not even come close. Has she ever managed anything?"

The discussion went back and forth for 30 minutes. In the end 4 of 13 board members present believed Harold was the right candi-date, 6 were strongly for Helen, and 3 seemed to be undecided. Joan stood up and provided a quick summary of the discussion. She con-tinued, "Before I call for a vote let me say that I agree with many of the concerns about Helen. Many valid concerns have been raised about the potential impact of her inexperience. If we hire her, we will need to provide hands-on support to her in the areas where she lacks experience. For example, one area is HR. As the chair of the HR com-mittee, I will commit to meeting with her weekly to provide her guid-ance not only in HR but also in managing her staff. She is going to have to make some difficult decisions about some of the staff. For financial guidance I have asked Paulette, the chair of our finance committee, if she would do the same."

"Franklin, as president of Mission City University, has agreed to serve as a mentor to her and meet with her regularly to guide her overall development as a leader. He has committed to connecting her to other faculty members who can provide additional support."

> Joan continued, "We may call on other board members to provide support on specific projects. The organization has many things that need to be fixed; we will look to the board for volunteers when needed. This extra support is just temporary."
>
> The board voted 10 to 3 to hire Helen. Two of the board members who voted against her resigned from the board.
>
> The next morning Hank and Joan offered Helen the job. They expressed confidence she was going to provide outstanding leadership but were clear about the areas she needed to grow. Hank shared the board's plan to provide support. Helen was excited and ready to dig in. Joan indicated that they would review her performance at the end of every three months during her first year.

Mission-Driven CPOs

Is being fanatic about mission something people can develop and nurture in themselves or do you either have it or not? I believe passion for mission can be nurtured. But being mission-driven requires a full understanding of the roots of your passion and a willingness to examine your beliefs. I asked the leaders I interviewed the origin of their passion for mission. There were two common answers.

First, it came from their parents and grandparents, who had been teachers, social workers, police officers, volunteers, and donors. The family instilled a belief in making a difference in the world that led them to a career in social services.

The second biggest influence on being mission-driven stems from their actual experience of being personally helped. They may have grown up with some challenges that they overcame thanks to someone who encouraged them and helped them find a path to success. Similarly, someone in their family received assistance that made a difference. Many of these leaders feel there is no way they can ever repay the people who helped them or their family, but they dedicated their life to making a difference to others.

Effective leaders can tell an inspiring story about the mission. They are able to weave their personal experience together with the story of their mission to create an inspiring and compelling narrative. This doesn't just happen. Effective leaders spend hours organizing their thinking. Here are some questions to help you get started:

- What is your mission origin story? How does it influence your passion for the organization's mission?
- Why is the mission of your organization important? What difference will it make for individuals, for the community, and for the country? What data do you have to support your impact?
- What are some compelling change stories of people or circumstances that capture the power of your mission?

Use the Fanatical About Mission Worksheet in the Resource Center to guide developing your own compelling mission story.

My Mission Origin Story

My father's life story is the origin of my passion for mission. He was a high school teacher, coach, and later the vice principal. He grew up in the Depression and left home in 1942 at age 15 to enlist (he changed his birth certificate from 1927 to 1925 so he could enlist). He felt the military gave him discipline and a sense of purpose. An officer recognized his potential and encouraged him to go to college when the war ended. He was probably one of the few teachers and vice principals who dropped out and never graduated high school but did graduate college. Throughout his career he reached out to the kids who were struggling the most and helped them to see their potential. Many reached out to him throughout their life to say thank you and continue to seek his guidance. I did not realize I had the same drive to serve until I was an adult and had an opportunity to experience firsthand what it was like to make a difference in someone's life.

In graduate school I went for an interview for an internship at the South Philadelphia Community Center. Jerry Romeo, the center director, was extremely mission-driven. The entire staff continuously talked about what could be done to make a difference for individual children and families, and how to make the programs more impactful. I knew I wanted to be part of that mission-driven culture. When I joined the staff of Boys & Girls Clubs of America it was inspiring to know that every day all across America thousands of people were dedicating themselves to the mission of enabling all young people, especially those who need us most, to reach their full potential as productive, caring, responsible citizens.

Notes for Board Members

Many board members articulated the challenge of hiring a CPO who is a good manager and administrator and can excite people about the organization's mission. Larger organizations may have the resources to hire an experienced mission-driven leader with proven expertise in fund raising, board development, and financial leadership and with the business acumen leaders need to succeed. These organizations also have the resources to hire specialists to lead resource development, finance, HR, and operations. But for smaller organizations with limited infrastructure the CPO must do it all. These organizations need to decide what is most important. Do they hire someone who has demonstrated management experience? Or do they look for a CPO with an insatiable drive to achieve the organization's mission?

Here is how some board members described their choice:

We can teach the technical pieces of the job, but some qualities like belief in the mission, drive, work ethic, and integrity cannot be taught. We need to hire for these first.

Passion was the main thing that set our CPO apart. She had a presence that was uplifting. An incredibly positive approach to leadership. The board had to ask, did we want an administrator or someone who would be a strong presence in the community? We could not picture some of the more qualified candidates being the leader the organization needed. Her positive approach was refreshing.

Initially some board members leaned toward hiring a competent administrator. But in the end, we opted for someone that excited us.

It can be hard to articulate what you are looking for until you meet the right person. The reasons we hired her are not generally in the job description. In the end the board determined we needed a big picture thinker who was willing to partner with the board to learn together.

I asked every CPO and board member about the hiring process. I was curious about how and why the board selected the CPO and what lessons there were for other organizations. Focusing first on hiring a CPO who was fanatical about mission and driven to make a difference was an unexpected finding. In fact, it may be the single most important concept to take away from this book. I believe it applies to every nonprofit. Based on my conversations with board members, here are my recommendations to board members about hiring a CPO:

- First, identify the people who are excited by the mission and have an insatiable desire to make a difference. These are the core leadership attributes most needed for success. The Resource Center at the back of the book suggests questions you might ask to explore how candidates view the mission of your organization (See Board Member Guide to Hiring and Onboarding Your CPO in the Resource Center).
- Second, determine if the person has the capacity to learn and develop the skills needed for the organization to operate efficiently. If the board believes they can develop expertise to manage the organization, the board must determine how they will support and grow the CPO. Even larger organizations with the resources to hire an experienced mission-driven leader should carefully assess the areas the leader will need support and to grow into the leader the organization needs.

- Third, once the CPO is selected the board needs to establish a thorough onboarding plan. This is essential and often overlooked. In a small organization where there is little if any infrastructure to support critical functions such as finance, HR, technology, or resource development the board must work in partnership with the CPO to ensure these are well managed. Board members must help the CPO to grow in these areas through hands-on coaching to the CPO and by directly supplementing and supporting these functions as needed. As the organization grows and reliable systems and practices are put in place, board members can begin to play a smaller role. For smaller nonprofits to succeed, this direct support to operations by board members may be the difference between success or failure.

Here are some examples of the advice board members suggested for hiring and onboarding a CPO:

- Hire a good CPO and work hard to make them successful. Board members must sometimes serve as mentors and partners.
- There wasn't much in place structurally. The board recognized the staff was small with little capacity to support infrastructure such as finance, resource development or HR. The board committed to put in a massive number of hours to provide that support. For example, the donor list, vendor list, and membership list were all a mess. Board members came and spent hours cleaning them up. The board had to do this; there was no other choice. Additionally, we completely rewrote the bylaws for board governance. They had not changed in 40 years.
- The CPO we hired did not have experience in HR and finance. We outsourced these functions to a community foundation before hiring the CPO. Over time, as the organization grew and added a CFO, and we brought finances back into the organization.
- Staff were doing multiple jobs as we did not have resources for sufficient infrastructure. The board filled in the gaps where we did not have staff expertise.

- The CPO did not have experience in HR and finance. We assigned a board member as financial coach and another board member as [an] HR coach. The board chair spent considerable time with the CPO in the first few months to help navigate the changes that needed to be made and support their growth as a leader.
- The board believed the new CPO could think long term and could handle the things that needed to be addressed in the short term with support from the board. The board established a plan to provide the new CPO with support and mentoring. The board designated:
  - A board member with a financial background to help organize, set up, and monitor financial systems
  - An attorney to support human resources
  - A university president to mentor the CPO to support her growth as a leader
  - An engineer to support planning and construction of a new facility

CPOs recognized the value of board's support. One CPO shared how she leaned on the board for help. She needed to remove some staff; the board provided support and HR advice. Board members accompanied her to her first meeting with every funder. The chair of the finance committee went over the finances with her once a month.

Resource Center for Truth 1

The following resources are available in the Resource Center at the end of the book and available online:

- Board Member Guide to Hiring and Onboarding the CPO
- Fanatical About Mission Worksheet
- Preparing a 100-Day Plan
- Sample 100-Day Plan
- CPO Guide to Building Relationships Conversation Starters
- Suggested Questions for Initial Meetings with Individual Board Members

2

Truth 2: Fix, Stabilize, or Replace Systems, Practices, and People Who Are Not Working

"Change will not come if we wait for some other person or some other time. We are the ones we've been waiting for. We are the change that we seek."

Barack Obama

I believe this observation is true for all leaders. If you are a board member or staff leader in an organization, the opportunity to change and transform the organizations you lead into a powerful force that changes lives, saves lives, achieves incredible results, and lifts entire communities is always there for you. But the journey to excellence requires a deep and fanatical commitment to mission. It requires the audacity to declare your intention to insist on excellence in every corner of the organization. It requires the discipline to never accept good enough. It requires unwavering belief and optimism in the capacity of the organization to continuously expand and improve. And it requires a commitment to make decisions, big and small, to support your mission-driven aspirations.

Transformational leaders always believe the door is open. They begin making needed changes almost immediately. There are two critical areas that demand attention:

- First, they recognize that transformation begins by ensuring the organization operates with optimal efficiency and effectiveness. Transformational leaders establish systems, standards,

29

process, and practices that govern day-to-day operations. They recognize they cannot make progress if they must spend too much of their time solving problems, managing every detail of operations, and resolving endless crises.

- Second, they establish and communicate expectations for staff performance and behavior. Staff members who cannot meet the standards are replaced.

Let's see how Helen is making changes as the new CPO of the Community Centers of Mission City.

Helen's First Board Meeting as CPO

At Helen's first board meeting 11 of 13 board members are in attendance. The board is eager to hear from Helen. They are seeking confirmation they made the right decision. Helen's goal is to provide an honest assessment of the organization and gain a commitment to act.

Board chair Hank Salvan calls the meeting to order. After a few short committee reports, he calls on Helen to give the CPO report. He introduces Helen by praising the job she has done. "Helen has accomplished a great deal in five weeks. I am confident she is the leader we need to strengthen our operations, increase our impact, and enable us to grow. Helen the floor is yours."

Helen stands and moves to the front of the room. "First, I want to thank all of your for your help, support, and guidance. Your enthusiasm, dedication, and commitment to our mission is one of our greatest assets. In the past five weeks I have talked with the following people:

- Every board member including the two who resigned
- All full- and part-time staff members
- Leadership of the community advisory committees from each of our Community Centers
- Key funders, including a meeting with United Way that Hank and Harold Starmon, our resource development committee chair, attended with me

"I have learned a great deal. It is hard to know where to begin. I am not going to sugarcoat anything. I know you are very aware we have challenges. With your continued help and support, I am confident we can make progress quickly. There are several changes we need to make immediately. Our facilities are a mess and there are safety concerns especially at the Southside Center. I have made a few changes already to address safety, routine maintenance, record keeping, and our program. I have asked the Center directors to begin preparing a weekly program plan. We have raised expectations across the board, and some of our staff members may not be able to embrace and implement the changes we are making.

"I am going to call on the chairs of the facilities, planning, finance, and human resources committees to add their perspective and outline next steps."

The minutes of the meeting reflected the following:

Facilities and Safety Committee. At Helen's suggestion, the facilities committee conducted an inspection of our buildings. The Southside Center is in terrible condition. There are major safety concerns that need immediate attention. Routine maintenance has been deferred for years. The roof leaks, causing an outbreak of mold on the second floor. Only half the toilets work, there is graffiti on the outside of the building, and every room needs painting, decorating, and a thorough cleaning. Beverly Vartson, chair of the facilities committee, proposed closing the building for one week to clean, paint, and repair what they could. Board members committed to work two days to help clean the building and make minor repairs. The committee committed to recruit others to volunteer. Beverly reported that her office will close one day during the week so her staff can spend the day working at the Center. "It will be a team-building activity for us," she stated. Two other board members committed to bringing a team from their office for a workday. Beverly will work with staff in advance to organize the work and make sure needed supplies are available.

Board chair Hank Salvan and Helen have secured a commitment from the Mission City Building Company to provide cleaning supplies, paint, and other materials to make routine repairs. Mission City Building Company will also encourage their employees to volunteer at least one day. An appeal to the Community Foundation for an emergency grant to repair the roof and fix the plumbing has been made. The foundation director will tour the building tomorrow.

Strategic Planning Committee. Systems or standard practices to govern daily operations need to be fully developed. The United Way has expressed concern over inaccuracy in the reporting of our membership and participation records. Helen is keeping a list of everything she discovers that needs to be addressed and has begun working with staff members to formalize new processes in writing. Francis Stillman, chair of the planning committee, will provide additional support to Helen to assess what is needed and help create written policies and procedures to guide routine practices. The strategic planning committee proposed that each board committee assess the area of operations they oversee. The committee will provide a progress report at the next board meeting.

Finance Committee. Paulette Nelson, finance committee chair, reported that she believes they now have a good picture of the organization's finances. We have a budget of $912,000, we are $250,000 in debt, and we have reached the limits of our current line of credit. There is an immediate need for cash to make our next payroll. We will receive the next reimbursement from the government for our childcare and senior citizen meal program in four weeks. In the meantime, we will ask the bank to increase our line of credit.

Resource Development Committee. Harold Starmon, chair of the resource development committee, provided an update on the organization's first annual campaign. Between now and our next meeting he and Hank will be talking to each board member to secure their gift and establish a list of the individuals they will solicit. He asked that board members make their gifts right away to help ease their current cash flow challenges. The next board meeting will include training and preparation for board members to solicit gifts.

__Human Resources Committee.__ Chair of the human resources committee Leslie Silver has been working with Helen to develop HR policies and procedures. She reported that staff member files are incomplete, there are few current performance plans or reviews, and in one case key documents are missing. Some staff members are pushing back at the structure and accountability Helen is establishing to improve day-to-day operations. Helen has begun documenting her concerns and is prepared to act.

Helen concluded her report to the board: "Everyone I meet tells me how important our Centers are to Mission City. They know we are struggling and are worried about our future. There are many things that need attention, but the biggest change needs to be in the quality of the programs and services we provide. This begins with a focus on safety and security. There are many improvements we can make to our ongoing operations that will make our Centers safe places with the capacity to make a difference for the families who live in the communities we serve. We will turn things around, but there are some difficult decisions to be made in the days ahead."

Helen recognized that before an organization can grow and transform it must stabilize day-to-day operations by establishing systems, processes, and standard practices that are universally implemented across the organization. These are the basic ingredients for well-managed organizations that operate efficiently.

Fix and Stabilize Systems and Practices

In his book *Think Big Act Small* Jason Jennings begins the chapter on letting go with advice from Dennis Higsby, former CPO of Cabalas. "If something isn't working, fix it[;] if it can't be fixed, then get rid of it" (Jennings, 2012, p. 61).

This is excellent advice. Leaders must be vigilant about addressing what is not working. Once something is broken or obsolete and not addressed, it becomes the status quo. People work around it even though it requires extra time and energy and takes the focus away from mission.

To be successful and compete for resources nonprofit organizations must be well managed and operate efficiently. This is a particular challenge for most nonprofits because so much of their resources are dedicated directly to mission. There is frequently little if any dedicated administrative support for functions such as finance, human resources, technology, or even resource development. The CPO and staff members, with support from the board members, handle many administrative tasks related to resource development, finance, human resources, record keeping, maintenance, collection of data for reporting, outcome measurement, and myriad other ongoing daily tasks that keep the organization running.

Leaders, especially new leaders, must look at everything with a critical eye. Many of the leaders interviewed described their primary role early in their tenure as "chief problem-solver." There either were few systems or the systems that existed were inadequate. One board member described the state of the organization when the transformational leader was hired as a hot mess. There were few standard processes; the CPO had to direct every decision.

Most of the organizations interviewed were struggling or just "doing okay," neither growing or declining, when the leader who transformed the organization was hired. Some had a leader who initially prospered, but could not take the organization further. This led to an organization that became stagnant, stuck in place. Others had not been able to find the right leader and had experienced a high degree of CPO turnover. A couple had a leadership change at a time when the organization had a significant growth opportunity that required a different structure and a different leadership style to succeed. All required significant change if they were to thrive and grow. Here is how CPOs described the situation during their first few months:

- It was really crazy. No job descriptions. No files. I spent the first month just figuring out what was going on.
- You can't change and grow the organization until you stabilize everything. Otherwise, it is hard to know what to do. New leaders must move quickly. Three key areas for me were finance, safety, and staff.
- It was all a mess, [with] not many things working. I took things on one at a time. I solved one problem and went on to the next thing.

- We started by cleaning up membership records. I put a membership tracking system and process in place. This included software and clear direction to staff about expectations for having accurate, timely information.
- When I was hired the organization was not very sophisticated. We did not have much data; everyone was doing their own thing. We began to standardize process, organize information, and develop systems for all areas of operations.
- The organization had grown fast, from a few employees to over 50. We needed policy and process to operate more efficiently and effectively than we did when we were smaller.
- You can't solve all the problems right away. I took the first few weeks to figure things out, establish a plan, and start chipping away. I asked people for help and made sure I understood the finances.
- You can't change and grow the organization until you stabilize. Otherwise, it is difficult to know what to do.

Despite the challenges and the stress, many CPOs recalled these early months as fun and exciting. Fun and exciting? How could difficult challenges and stress also be fun:

- It was really crazy. No job description. No files. I spent the first month just figuring out what was going on. I created a document of "critical information" so I could keep track of everything that needed to be addressed. It was fast-paced; every day looked different and was mentally and physically challenging. But I liked that we were solving problems—every day it felt like we moved forward. I loved it.
- My goal was to get an understanding of what was going on. I needed to understand our financial position and where revenue was coming from. I did not know how bad it was until I was on the job for a few weeks. We had a big deficit and no cash position. On day seven I was served papers by the IRS—we were being audited. We resolved to start operating like a business. It was rewarding to see progress. This was the most fun I ever had.

- Initially I had to be really in the weeds solving and fixing problems. This was fulfilling as every day we got tangibly better. I still struggle with thinking I must do it all. At some point I had to learn to give up control.
- There was a lot to do, and it was fun.

Board members saw the same challenges. The following quotes highlight that their biggest concern was about finances:

- Initially we [the board] had to be involved to support basic organizational functions as staff did not have specialized expertise. For example, because our finances needed to be addressed, I recruited a friend who was CFO of a large company to identify the core issues we needed to address.
- It was all a mess; not many things were working. Our CPO took things one at a time, solved [it,] and went on to the next thing.
- Our CPO led with mission then acknowledged the need to fix some problems and told people how they could help.
- We did not have adequate financial controls.
- Our organization did not have proper financial structure. The board had to ask how we can build structure around our CPO so she can be successful.
- The CPO carefully went through the books and established a plan to stabilize our finances.
- We conducted a self-assessment process. This brought issues to light that the organization needed to address. It was very revealing about what we needed to work on. The assessment process enabled the board to discuss the challenges the organization faced. The assessment was the basis of our initial strategic plan with our new CPO. We needed to get basics in place.

Before an organization can grow it must first operate efficiently. Every organization, no matter how small, needs systems, process, and routines that ensure smooth, consistent, day-to-day operations. Some of these are straightforward, such as how the building gets locked up each evening, how the phone is answered, how files and records are kept, or how staff members account for their time. Others are more comprehensive, such as how the organization's finances are managed or what are our human resource policies and procedures and how are they carried out. The expectations for accountability and being an efficient well-managed organization are the same no matter the organization's size. Fixing, stabilizing, or replacing requires carrying out basic organizational functions to meet a high standard of excellence with the least amount of attention possible.

Without efficient operating systems, the leader becomes the source of all decisions big and small. Every day there are thousands of problems to solve, questions to answer, and things to do to keep the organization afloat. Leaders can become trapped in an endless cycle of problem-solving and providing direction for completing every task. They get caught in managing the day-to-day operational detail. This leaves little or no time to address the big things that can move the organization forward.

In smaller organizations the leader and the board must work together to carry out these changes. Board members may need to supplement staff capacity, especially early in the CPO's tenure and during times of rapid growth. Board members are a critical resource to the CPO and the organization especially at the beginning of their tenure. Here are some examples:

- Board volunteers volunteered to renovate a facility that had been neglected. They made personal commitments, recruited volunteers, and secured a gift to fund supplies and equipment. Staff mapped out all the jobs and projects so that small groups or individuals could be plugged into specific projects. This reinforced a message to the staff and the community that the organization was changing and created new opportunities.
- A volunteer from a local church asked what else they could do, and the CPO replied they could bring pizza for the kids one night a week. The volunteer agreed and now a group from this church meets once a week and prepares meals. There were 12,000 meals provided the first year. It has grown to 60,000 meals annually, all provided by volunteers.
- Board members converted a drawer full of business cards, notes with names and contact information, and lists of people who attended special events into a donor database.

- A board member who served as chief human resource officer for a hospital created a human resource policy manual for the organization, arranged for a legal review, and worked with the CPO to establish a plan to fully implement and communicate to staff members.
- A board member worked in partnership with the CPO to assess the organization's current financial position, organize a financial management system, and develop sound financial practices.
- The organization had an opportunity to serve significantly more youth in partnership with schools, but they only had a few weeks to more than double the size of their operation. Board members volunteered to register youth and parents and assist in hiring and orienting new staff members.
- The organization created a simple strategic plan that outlined strategic initiatives to stabilize, and grow in three areas: program, resources, and board. The theme was easily understood and clearly communicated the organization's commitment to do the following:
  - Stabilize and address current issues such as facilities, infrastructure, staffing, and program, and develop the systems and processes needed for the organization to operate efficiently and effectively.
  - Grow and drive greater impact.

This is the mindset needed to begin transformation. Organizations that have struggled need to stabilize and install systems and structure to operate smoothly. This is a prerequisite for growth. There is little time to grow and transform the organization if the leader must spend the whole day managing every aspect of operations, answering questions, and solving problems.

Make Needed People Changes

In *Good to Great* author Jim Collins addressed the importance of having the right people as "if we can get the right people on the bus, the right people in the right seats, and the wrong people off the bus, then we'll figure out how to take us someplace great" (Collins, 2001, p. 41).

Fixing what is not working applies to people as well as systems and process. Collins, who also wrote *Good to Great and the Social Sector* (2005) and other best-selling leadership books, spoke at Boys & Girls Clubs of America's National Conference. Dr. Collins was an amazing speaker. Everyone in the room was inspired by his remarks and how he made his research relevant to the everyday work of leading a nonprofit organization. Following his keynote presentation there was a breakout session that provided an opportunity for a dialogue with Dr. Collins. About halfway through the session he stopped and noted that almost all the questions were about getting the "right people on the bus and the wrong people off the bus." He thought for a moment, then shared his belief that this must be a priority. Without the right staff team, the organization is stuck in mediocrity.

In the *Good to Great and Social Sector* monograph, Collins notes that great organizations "focused on getting and hanging on to the right people in the first place—those who are productively neurotic, those who are self-motivated and self-disciplined, those who wake up every day, compulsively driven to do the best they can because it is simply part of their DNA" (Collins, 2005, p. 15). You can't have a great nonprofit organization without great people.

This begins with the board hiring a CPO that fits this description. Then the board must support the CPO in building a team of mission-driven zealots. This process may begin by parting company with staff members who do not fit this description. In a small nonprofit with few employees every person is especially critical to success. Each person represents a substantial portion of the organization's resources. Every staff person must have the following qualities:

- Be deeply committed to the organization's mission
- Possess an insatiable desire to make a difference
- Have the basic skills the position requires and be committed to continuously building their skills and knowledge
- Be able to work collaboratively as part of a team

The first step is often "getting the wrong people off the bus." This is often a turning point for the organization and the CPO. A short time into her tenure Helen had to deal with a staff person who ignored some of the policies and procedures she had put in place. Let's see how Helen handled this.

Two Weeks after Helen's First Board Meeting

At one time the Southside Community Center was the hub of the community. People remember when it was filled with activity from early morning to late in the evening. This was no longer true; participation was at an all-time low. Several of their traditional partners were no longer using the Center as their base of operations. The current Center Director, Peter Kannon, had been there for five years. Helen was unsure if he was going to succeed. She had been visiting the Center at least twice a week to observe and learn more about the operation. She had urged Peter to reach out to the community to increase participation. A small increase in attendance was reported, but whenever she visited the building seemed empty. Helen insisted that several practices be changed to ensure the Center was a safe, welcoming place. This included assigning a staff person to the front entrance to greet every person, to monitor who was entering, to keep track of participation, and to better supervise the entrance lobby.

Next week the Southside Center will close for a facility makeover led by the board. Ultimately the building needed a significant upgrade or to be replaced. It will be difficult to demonstrate the need for a significant investment with the present level of participation. But the building needed some immediate attention.

Helen made an unannounced visit to each facility every few days. Tonight Helen arrived at the Southside Community Center at about 6:30 pm. There was no one at the front entrance. There were fewer than 25 people in the building. A few teens were playing basketball in the gym while the staff person in the gym was talking on his cell phone. There was a class for new mothers being led by a nurse from a local hospital. And there were a half dozen people in the lounge. The staff person in the lounge was watching the news and didn't acknowledge Helen when she entered the room. She could not find Center director Peter Kannen or the program director Marcus Maze. The part-time staff person in the lounge thought they went to get something to eat. Helen found an attendance tracking sheet and went to each room to record attendance, then she sat behind the front desk to monitor and record participation, monitor the entrance, and wait for Peter to return.

Thirty minutes later Peter and Marcus returned. Helen asked Marcus to take over the front desk while she talked with Peter. When they got to Peter's office Helen believed she smelled alcohol on his breath.

Helen said, "I am not sure what is going on. I am very concerned no one is supervising the front entrance. We agreed we needed a record of who was in the building and for safety we needed to monitor who was entering the building. When I walked around, I could only find two staff members—one was watching TV and the other one was talking on the phone. And, most of all, neither you nor Marcus were here. Our policy is that a full-time staff is always present when the building is open. I also smell alcohol on your breath."

Peter replied defensively, "Two part-time staff are absent; they called in sick. It was a busy day; Marcus and I had not had a chance to eat. It was quiet. I suggested we step out for a quick bite, and, yes, I had one beer with my sandwich. Nothing bad happened, did it?"

Helen fought to keep her anger in check when she asked, "Do you believe it is okay to leave the building open with no one at the front desk and only two part-time staff in the building? What if something had happened? What if someone had gotten hurt?

"Look, I'm sorry. It won't happen again," Peter replied.

Helen was concerned about Peter's performance from the beginning. She had difficulty engaging him in a conversation about his goals for the Center. She had stressed the importance of safety from her first day. She was worried he wouldn't be able to pull together the upcoming facility renovation the board was planning. She had talked to Hank, and he advised her to make sure she clearly defined and communicated her expectations and documented her concerns. She determined now was the time to begin. She took a deep breath and said, "This Center needs a director who is driven to make a difference. I know you have roots in the community, but I am not sure you are the right person to lead this Center."

Peter stood up towering over Helen before replying angrily. "What do you mean I am not the right person? Who the hell are you to tell me what this Center needs? You have never worked here; you know nothing about being a director. Get out of here so I can get to work!"

Helen had intended to only have a conversation with Peter to express her concerns, and probably put something in writing as follow-up in the morning. But it felt like a line had been crossed. She knew the organization would be better off without Peter. "It means you are not going to be able to continue to be part of this organization," she replied.

"You are firing me?" Peter asked in disbelief.

"Yes," replied Helen.

Peter responded by cursing her out in a loud voice. "You can't do this; I was here before you. You will be sorry you messed with me. You are ruining this organization with all your rules and expectations."

When he was finished Helen asked, "Please give me your keys. I will stay and close the building. Your employment is ending effective today. I will have a letter and your final check ready for you tomorrow. Call me to let me know if you want to pick it up or if I should put it in the mail. We can arrange a time for you to pack up your belongings when the Center is not open."

Peter threw his keys on the floor and left the building.

After talking with Marcus, Helen called board chair Hank Salvan to share what happened. He was supportive but indicated that he wished she had sent Peter home and then met with him tomorrow after the board was aware of what she planned to do. "We will help you write a termination letter, but we should give him the opportunity to resign. I will contact Leslie Silver (chair of the HR committee) and we will connect with you first thing in the morning."

Helen asked, "Did I do the right thing? Maybe he deserved another chance."

"Don't look back," Hank advised. "There was a better way to handle this, but it would have eventually ended up with the same result. I will see you in the morning."

Helen replied, "I will be going in early and moving my office to the Southside Center. I will serve as the Center director until we can hire *someone." The next morning with input from Hank and Leslie, Helen prepared a termination letter. She attempted to contact Peter to give him the option of resigning, but he refused to take her calls. A day later, board members, many of the organization's donors, the staff, leaders in the Southside Community, elected officials, and local media received the following email from Peter. Peter also posted a copy of the email on Instagram and Facebook.*

To: Friends of the Community Centers of Mission City
From: Peter Kannon, Former Director of the Southside Community Center
Subject: The demise of our cherished organization
I grew up in the southside of Mission City and have been involved with the Southside Community Center since I was 11 years old. I worked there part-time while in college and have been a full-time staff person for over 10 years, the last five years as Center director. I love the work the Community Center does. I believe deeply in the mission of the organization. It made a difference for me and my family. Every day I see the impact it has on the community.
Three days ago, I was fired by the new CPO, Ms. Helen Foster. I received nothing in writing. No warning, no justification, just clean out your office, turn in your keys, and get out.
Our Centers make a difference for many struggling families. I am genuinely concerned about the future of the Community Centers of Mission City. Ms. Foster has little experience as a leader. She does not understand our work. She is more concerned about policies and paperwork than the life-changing services we provide. She is impulsive and makes rash decisions. Many of the staff and people in the community share my concerns.
Thank you to everyone for all you do for families and children in our community.

A story about Peter that included a copy of Peter's email appeared in a weekly community newspaper a few days later.

All leaders face difficult choices about resource allocation, strategy, and how to handle a crisis, but choices about people are arguably the most difficult. In their book *The Cycle of Leadership*, Noel Tichy and Nancy Cardwell (2002) emphasize the need for leaders to have "edge." They define edge "as the ability to make difficult yes-no calls" (p. 93). A leader's edge comes from a clear understanding of what they want to accomplish, and for nonprofit organizations this begins with mission.

Making tough decisions about people is the most difficult part of being a leader. Even when the grievances are severe it can be difficult to act. Leaders do not relish this part of their job. In Chapter 1, I stated that belief in mission gives leaders the courage and will to make tough calls. Your organization's mission demands board and professional leaders willing to make calls about the people your organization needs to succeed. Putting mission first provides clarity and demands that the leader act.

At many of the organizations benchmarked, the CPO made personnel changes in the first few months and in some cases in the first week. These changes were a powerful statement by the new leader. They signaled to everyone that standards and expectations were changing. Here is how CPOs summarized the changes they made:

- I had to make staff changes right away. We kept staff [who] bought into the mission and the goals of our program.
- I asked two people to leave on the first day—one was talking on the phone while driving a bus, the other was taking a nap. We had a new leadership team in a few months. This signaled to everyone there were new standards.
- Having the right people is the key. We had many people challenges in the beginning.
- We had three full-time staff and six part-time. Only one staff person was still there after six months.
- We had to rebuild; we had a completely new leadership team within six months.
- The director of development and operations agreed to move on.
- The board was aware the organization was not doing well. They were aware enough to get rid of the previous CPO, but probably not fully aware about how bad things were.

- As we have grown, we have restructured. Some people have been promoted and others have not. It can be hard for everyone to understand but we have to do what is best for the organization and our mission.

A colleague I once worked with defined ethics for nonprofit leaders as "making tough decisions about the use of scarce resources." By his definition, it is unethical to keep staff members who are not buying in and not producing results. The ethics of being a leader demands we use every dollar people invest in the organization to achieve the maximum amount possible to achieve the mission. By that definition, failure by leaders to take decisive steps to address performance issues may be unethical.

I have observed many organizations that have one or two people underperforming who have been there a long time. They may have been valued contributors at one time, but as the organization grew and expectations changed, they were not able to develop the skills or mindset to grow with the organization. Sometimes they are moved to a meaningless job where they are out of the way and do little harm. It is a mistake and a waste of scarce resources to create a position you would not usually have to accommodate a staff person not able to provide value. How can this be justified to the people and organizations that provide resources?

Ruthless Leadership?

When I was a social work graduate student, I had the good fortune to work with Jeff Ball. Jeff had recently completed an appointment as Deputy Secretary for Children and Youth in the Pennsylvania Department of Welfare. Jeff was a superior teacher. We had an ongoing discussion about the need for people leading social service organizations to be in his words "more ruthless."

The idea of a leader being ruthless did not feel right to me, but I came to understand that he didn't mean ruthless in a brutal and cruel sense. He meant that mission supersedes everything. He believed that sometimes leaders who are deeply committed to helping others wait too long to address underperforming staff members rather than act decisively to address performance issues.

Beyond the ethical aspects of addressing performance issues, leaders who fail to address performance issues lose credibility in the organization. Once poor performance is accepted it becomes the standard. Staff members who are producing notice others who are not as mission focused. They begin to question why the leader does not act. Donors also sense the malaise in the organization. Transformational leaders fully embrace the mission, set high expectations, and act accordingly.

Community Centers of Mission City
Emergency Board Meeting
One Week Later

Board members were flooded with calls about the dismissal of Peter Kannon. Some supported Helen's decision, others demanded an explanation, and some called for Helen's dismissal. Peter's mother, a long-time community resident, called everyone she knew to complain. It was even picked up by a local TV news broadcast. Many stakeholders suggested the board conduct a full investigation.

Board chair Hank Salva asked Leslie Silver, chair of the HR committee, to lead an investigation. He also appointed Albert Sarandos, a long-time board member who was advocating for Helen's dismissal, and Sarah Williams, an attorney, to assist. He asked that they complete their investigation quickly. Because of the urgency, an emergency board meeting was scheduled. Many rumors were circulating. Some believed Helen would be fired. Helen wondered if she should resign and make it easier for all involved. The investigation committee provided the board with a written report with their recommendations in advance of the emergency meeting.

Hank Salvan called the meeting to order. "I know all of you are anxious to discuss the results of our investigation into the dismissal of Peter Kannon. Leslie, could you provide a summary of your findings?"

"I want to state at the beginning that we were unanimous in our recommendation," reported Leslie. "We believe Helen made the right decision in ending Peter Kannon's employment. There are some lessons learned for the board and for Helen, but if she had not acted, we would know we hired the wrong CPO. Our three major findings are as follows:

1. The Southside Community Center has had poor attendance and a growing loss of community support. The chair of their Community Advisory Committee was clear that he believed removing Peter was necessary.
2. Abandoning the building with only two part-time staff and no one staffing the entrance was unacceptable under any circumstances and clearly a violation of our policy.
3. Peter's response to Helen's questions was totally inappropriate and was probably fueled by alcohol.

"While we might have avoided the controversy if Helen had sent Peter home and then met with him the next day fully armed with the support of the board and prepared to offer him the opportunity to resign, it was absolutely the right decision to end his employment with us. Our recommendation is that we communicate our unequivocal support to Helen to the staff, our investors, and the community. If we want Helen to succeed, we need to give her the freedom to do her job and encourage her to build a team that is as mission-driven as she is. I believe it is safe to say this incident has been extremely difficult for her. She needs and deserves our support. We also need to help Helen learn and grow as a leader as a result of this incident."

When she finished Albert stood up to say, "As you know I was call-ing for Helen's dismissal when this first surfaced. After visiting the Center, talking to staff members, and interviewing others, I recog-nized I was wrong. I move that we express our formal support to Helen in writing and encourage every board member to communi-cate their support to Helen personally."

The minutes of the meeting reflected a unanimous vote of confidence for Helen and the actions she took. The board established a list of stake-holders each member would call to share their commitment to growing the organization under Helen's capable leadership. Every board member called Helen in the next few days to personally communicate their sup-port. This served as a powerful message to the staff members and all stakeholders about where the organization was headed.

Removing people isn't easy. It should always be done judiciously and compassionately. If expectations are clear and performance-focused feed-back is provided, dismissal should not be a surprise to the employee or the board.

Caution: Solving Problems Can Be Addictive

A word of caution: Leaders sometimes get stuck in the role of "chief problem-solver." Fixing things, solving problems, answering everyone's questions feels rewarding. Problems are being solved; you are making a difference.

Leaders who are good at getting things done are comfort-able being directly involved in day-to-day decisions. The dan-ger is that staff members become dependent on the leader to solve every problem. The result is a leader that spends most of the day directly engaged in managing operations. Initially this may be essential. But the goal must be to establish operating systems and mechanisms that ensure smooth operations with minimal daily direction from the leader. Transformational leaders develop people with the skills, knowledge, and judgment to solve the majority of operational challenges.

Summary

Fixing and stabilizing requires the right systems and process. It is difficult to focus on forward-looking strategic initiatives if the leader must spend all day, every day, solving operational and people problems. The more efficiency created, the more energy available for advancing the mission. Until the organization begins to operate smoothly and efficiently and has the right people the leader is stuck focusing on orchestrating daily operations. Once day-to-day operations begin to operate smoothly and the right people are on board, the leader can devote more attention to developing and communicating a strategy for moving forward.

Establishing systems and processes that enable the organization to operate efficiently requires an intentional focus and follow-through to change norms. Transformational leaders encourage feedback and suggestions about how to increase efficiency and effectiveness of operating mechanisms, but they stand strong so that policy, process, and procedures will be followed. Transformational leaders implement the basic stuff exceptionally well:

- They establish systems and practices for the organization to operate smoothly and efficiently and ensure they are followed.
- They set standards and expectations for staff members and hold them accountable.
- They find and hire people who believe in the mission and are driven to make a difference.

There is nothing revolutionary about this. Every leader can master these basics of leading an organization. So why doesn't this happen in every organization? It can only happen if board and staff leadership have the "edge" to make the difficult decisions and "edge" begins with a commitment to always act on behalf of the mission.

Notes to Board Members

In terms of fixing, stabilizing, or replacing systems, practices, and people who are not working, board members have four primary roles:

- **Provide support and expertise to organizational functions such as HR, finance, marketing, IT, and resource development.** Small organizations are unlikely to have staff expertise in these operating mechanisms. Board members can provide expertise and information the organization needs to thrive. This can be organized by board committees with some overall coordination by the board chair. The key for the board is assessing the status of the systems and of the CPO's experience and expertise. The board then develops a plan to provide the support needed along with clear expectations for the CPO's role. It may be necessary for board members to serve as volunteers to do some of the work while systems and practices are being developed.

- **Annually assess organizational operations to refine, update, and improve operations.** One step the board and staff members can take in partnership is an annual assessment of the organization's operations. Board members bring their expertise and external perspective. Staff members bring their knowledge of day-to-day operations. Together that can determine where and how the organization can improve operations. An annual assessment is also an opportunity to engage other stakeholders with specific expertise. In the Resource Center, Resources for Board and Staff Members to Assess and Build Systems, Practices, and Policies contains links to assessment tools for nonprofit organizations. Most of the tools listed provide standards for effective and efficient operating mechanisms.

- **Provide support to the CPO in managing people.** In addition to establishing HR policy and practices, someone on the board should have an ongoing conversation with the CPO about staff ability and performance. This is especially important at the beginning of the CPO's tenure. If the organization is not operating at an optimal level, anticipate the need for staff changes and discuss how they should be handled up front. This will not make them any easier, but it may eliminate some of the challenges that could arise. There are two major lessons from what happened to Helen and the Mission City Community Centers when she terminated Peter's employment:
  - First, be proactive about having initial and ongoing conversations with the CPO about staff performance and changes that could be necessary.
  - Second, the board must support the CPO when she makes changes. Many of the CPOs I interviewed went through situations similar to Helen's. The CPO was not always confident the board was going to be supportive. In the end these situations ended up being a turning point for the organization. The board understood the CPO had to lead the organization and the board's role was to provide the support needed for them to be successful.
- **Supervise and mentor the CPO.** This is an important board responsibility and it is too often overlooked. Generally, the board chair owns the primary responsibility, but the chair of each committee should be providing direction and feedback to the CPO regarding their function. This begins with establishing written annual goals and performance standards for the CPO and an annual performance review process.

Resource Center for Truth 2

The following resources are available in the Resource Center at the end of the book and will be available online:

- Resources for Board and Staff Members to Assess and Build Systems, Practices, and Policies
- Resources for Board and Staff Members to Support Human Resource Management
- Worksheet to Identify What Systems, Practices, and Policies Need to Be Fixed, Repaired, or Replaced
- Suggested Interview Questions Related to Mission and Motivation

3

Truth 3: Establish a Mission-Driven Strategy

"Strategy is not the consequence of planning, but the opposite; it is the starting point."

Henry Mintzberg

Achieving visionary outcomes is extremely difficult. There are no simple pathways to eliminating or reducing poverty, preventing or treating drug and alcohol abuse, keeping our environment pristine, providing comprehensive health care to everyone, enabling children from challenging circumstances to succeed, or to fix the myriad challenges we face as a nation that are addressed by the missions of nonprofit organizations. Transformational leaders succeed by clearly articulating and aligning organizations on a thoughtful, evidenced-informed strategy for how the organization will pursue its mission. Strategy is not the same as a strategic plan. As Mintzberg suggests, strategy is the starting point for planning. Strategy aligns, inspires, and guides decisions big and small. Strategy provides board and staff leaders with a clear understanding about these baseline issues:

- What difference the organization makes
- How the organization will operate to achieve superior results
- How the organization acquires resources

An effective strategy provides extraordinary clarity about how the organization achieves its mission. The best strategies are simple and easy to understand on the surface but complex underneath. The essence can be communicated in a few sentences. CPOs lead strategy development but all stakeholders provide input. Leaders "engage people in a journey. They lead in such a way that everyone on the journey helps shape its course" (Mintzberg, 1994). Here is how board members described the role of the CPO in strategy development:

- Every new CPO must realize everything starts with them. They must drive execution, develop new skill sets, and establish a vision that is written, clear, and inspiring. They need to be able to show the board, staff, donors, and other stakeholders how they are going to get there.
- Our CPO aligned everyone by simplifying a message about where we are going and how we will achieve superior results.
- The leader must have a truly clear picture of where we are currently and where we want to go. We need to know what the organization needs to look like today and in the future to succeed.

Let's check in to see how Helen is doing six months into her tenure as president and CPO of the Community Centers of Mission City.

Six Months Later
Community Centers of Mission City Board Retreat

For the past six months Helen has been primarily focused on solving myriad daily challenges. She has been busy repairing and replacing operating systems. With the board's support and assistance Helen has established systems, policies, and practices that enable the organization to operate efficiently. Every day is no longer an endless series of crises to be resolved. The organization is reaching more people. Relationships with major funders have improved and the board's first annual campaign provided new operating income to address some of the budget gaps. Helen is beginning to build a strong team.

She decided to hire a director of operations rather than fill the vacant resource development director position. There is a new director for the Southside Center who is building a strong program and repairing relationships with the community. Having achieved a level of stability, the organization is poised to move forward. But what is the next step?

Board chair Hank Salvan and Joan Fenz, chair of the search committee that hired Helen, met Helen for breakfast two weeks before the board retreat. This will be the first board retreat in many years. Hank and Joan commended Helen on the progress she is making. Joan said, "You have done great work; you have lifted the organization out of continuous crisis. We have achieved a level of stability that we desperately needed. Now we need to figure out what is next, and you must lead that discussion. This is going to require you to let go of many of the daily operations you have been focused on. Your most important role will become developing a strategy for how we succeed and then aligning the organization internally and externally on our strategy for success."

Hank added, "Your role must begin to evolve. We need a clear strategy for how we make a difference to the families and children of Mission City. To succeed you will need to delegate more responsibility for day-to-day operations and spend more time establishing and championing our mission strategy. The goal of the board retreat is to engage the board in a discussion about the future of the organization."

Helen was pleased that Hank and Joan recognized the progress they made but unsure about what she needed to do differently.

Summary of board retreat. *The board retreat was well attended, board members participated vigorously, and there was considerable optimism about the future. The discussion generated three themes for what the organization should focus on next:*

- ***Growth.*** *The board knew there were many people in need of the support that the community centers provide. Increasing the number of people reached will validate the impact of the community centers. This will increase their visibility and strengthen the case for resources.*

- **Replace or renovate their facilities.** *The need to invest significantly in either replacing or renovating their buildings was clear. The organization also needed more staff members in each building and to update its technology. Raising money to repair or replace their facilities is straightforward, understandable, and tangible. Many board members felt this was a good place to start.*
- **Focus on program and services to strengthen impact.** *The organization needs more clarity about the outcomes they achieve and how they make a difference. The board believed growth and new resources will follow if they are able to clearly articulate and demonstrate the difference the community centers make. Helen believed this is where the focus should be.*

The board discussed each of these possibilities but did not come to a conclusion. They asked Helen to work with the strategic planning committee to come back to the board with a recommendation about next steps. They suggested she seek input from some of their major donors, community leaders, and staff members. Overall, board members expressed optimism about the direction of the organization, but some were impatient. Board chair Salvan concluded, "We have made progress, but we have a long way to go. We need clarity about the next step. Our mission is important we need to keep moving."

Helen is excited about the board's enthusiasm, but unsure about what she needed to do next.

Some leaders can get stuck focusing all their energy on day-to-day operations. Once leaders establish systems, policies, and practices and a team to carry out daily operations, it is time to establish a clear, well-thought-out strategy for how the organization will achieve its mission. This requires leaders to engage every stakeholder in an ongoing dialogue. To be successful the CPO needs to facilitate and shape a strategy that incorporates everyone's input.

This strategy will affect all aspects of the organization, including structure, resource allocation, annual goals, board development, fund raising, and staff development. A mission-driven strategy enables leaders to develop a compelling story about how the organization makes a difference. Sharing this story over and over builds alignment, confidence, and energy across the organization and with every stakeholder.

And strategy begins with mission.

A Mission-Driven Strategy

In "Do Mission Statements Matter for Nonprofit Performance?" Pandy et al. (2017) state, "Passion for mission is crucial; however, passion alone cannot build and sustain organizations." Successful transformational leaders develop, articulate, and align the organization on a clear, evidence-informed strategy that provides clarity about how the organization will pursue its mission.

There are three components to a mission-driven strategy (Collins, 2005; Moore, 2000). Although I will present these components in a specific order, creating and building your organization's strategy is an ongoing dynamic process. Mission statements seldom change; strategy evolves based on the environment, the needs of the target population the organization serves, organizational learning, the capability of the staff and board members, and available resources. All aspects of a mission-driven strategy are interconnected and dependent on each other. Changing any part of your strategy affects the other components. In the previous three years many organizations had adopted a strategy to determine how to provide services during a pandemic. Strategy changed and evolved to reflect changing circumstances, but mission seldom changed.

Each of the three components of a mission-driven strategy requires leaders to answer a set of questions that clearly articulate how the organization will achieve its mission.

- **Mission strategy.** Mission strategy clearly defines who the organization will serve, what outcomes the organization delivers, and what services and programs will be provided to achieve these outcomes.
- **Organizational capability.** Transformational leaders determine what knowledge, skills, and information the organization needs

to implement its mission strategy. This includes a measurement plan to determine how well the organization is succeeding and how it can increase impact.

• **Resource acquisition.** Nonprofit organizations need resources to thrive. Transformational leaders establish a clear strategy for how they will build awareness and acquire the resources needed to deliver superior performance.

Strategy begins with mission. Nonprofits create value by pursuing the purpose expressed by their mission statement. Missions drive every decision. This may sound straightforward, but decisions often require trade-offs between competing ideas about what is most important. A mission-driven strategy establishes a shared understanding by all stakeholders of how the organization will achieve its mission. It enables leaders to prioritize and make difficult choices about services, programs, and allocation of resources.

Most mission statements have three parts:

• The difference the organization will make
• Who the organization will make a difference for
• How they will make a difference

Each part of the mission requires a clear, specific description of what the organization will do to achieve its mission. Consider the following missions of some familiar nonprofit organizations:

American Red Cross: The American Red Cross prevents and alleviates human suffering in the face of emergencies by mobilizing the power of volunteers and the generosity of donors.

- **Difference.** Prevent and alleviate human suffering
- **Who.** People experiencing an emergency
- **How.** Mobilize the power of volunteers and generosity of donors

Boys & Girls Clubs of America. To enable all young people, especially those who need us most, to reach their full potential as productive, caring, responsible citizens.

- **Difference.** Young people reaching their full potential as productive, caring, responsible citizens
- **Who.** All young people, especially those who need us most.
- **How.** Enable

Wings for Kids. To equip at-risk kids with the skills they need to succeed in school, stay in school, and thrive in life.

- **Difference.** Succeed in school, stay in school, and thrive in life
- **Who.** At-risk kids
- **How.** Equip kids with skills

Big Brothers/Big Sisters of America. To create and support one-to-one mentoring relationships that ignite the power and promise of youth.

- **Difference.** Ignite the power and promise of youth
- **Who.** Youth
- **How.** One-to-one mentoring relationships

AARP. To empower people to choose how they live as they age.

- **Difference.** People empowered to choose how they live
- **Who.** People who are aging
- **How.** Empower

Sierra Club. To practice and promote the responsible use of the earth's ecosystems and resources, to educate and enlist humanity to protect and restore the quality of the natural and human environment, and to use all lawful means to carry out these objectives.

- **Difference.** Protect and restore the quality of the natural and human environment
- **Who.** The natural and human environment (in this instance it is more what)
- **How.** Educate and enlist humanity to practice and promote responsible use of the earth's ecosystem and resources by all lawful means

These excellent examples of mission statements provide a general picture about the purpose of the organization. By design they are broad and leave considerable room for interpretation. They serve as the place to begin mapping out a strategy for how the organization will succeed.

Staff members and volunteers make hundreds of independent decisions every day. Without a clear, universally understood framework for these decisions, everyone creates their own personal strategy for achieving the organization's mission. Each person's interpretation affects how they make decisions about what outcomes are important, who they will serve, and what programs and services will make the biggest difference. This makes it extremely difficult to learn how to produce consistent results. Mission clarity enables organizations to align people, services, and organizational practices on a shared strategy for how the organization drives results (Berlan, 2018).

Board, staff members, volunteers, donors, and other stakeholders all need to be aligned around a clear agreed-upon understanding for how the organization pursues its mission. Mission clarity enables everyone to make decisions independently that are aligned with the organization's strategy for achieving its mission. Getting everyone aligned or on the same page is extremely important and takes an intentional, disciplined approach.

To clarify an organization's mission strategy, transformational leaders have three essential tasks:

- Clarify the difference the organization will make by defining specific outcomes.
- Identify who will be affected.
- Develop a service delivery model that clearly defines what services and programs will be provided.

Let's take a closer look at each of these tasks.

Clarify the difference the organization will make by defining specific outcomes. The mission statement expresses a broad outcome that will be achieved in the future in very general terms. Leaders need to articulate the outcomes in the present or near future. This provides clarity to everyone about the organization's impact. These near-term outcomes must logically lead to the longer-term outcome expressed in the mission statement and be grounded in research and evidence.

For example, The American Red Cross's long-term outcome expressed in the mission statement is "alleviates human suffering in the face of emergencies." According to their website an immediate outcome is "all people affected by disaster across the country and around the world receive care, shelter and hope." Shelter and care are clear outcomes. After a disaster, food, shelter, and medical care are the priority. Hope is a little more difficult to define and might take a little longer to achieve. However, hope might be defined as people who have experienced an emergency and have a plan and the means for restoring their home and rebuilding their community.

Let's take a detailed look at how Wings for Kids has done this. Wings for Kids was founded in 1996 as a one-week summer camp to empower girls in Charleston, SC. That fall they opened their first after-school program. Today Wings for Kids operates comprehensive after-school programs in four cites and provides training for teachers and youth development professionals nationwide. Wings for Kids is one of only a very few community-based organizations to have successfully conducted a random control trial (RCT) evaluation demonstrating their impact (Wings for Kids, n.d.a). When Bridgett Durkan Laird became CPO in 2011 Wings had a budget of approximately $1 million and a positive reputation in Charleston for quality programs. Today their budget is $4.5 million, and their reach extends across the country.

The outcome in their mission statement is "Kids with the skills they need to succeed in school, stay in school, and thrive in life."

Ask yourself: if you were tasked with achieving that outcome for "at-risk" kids, what would you do? There are many possible approaches to how you might support kids succeeding in school. You might offer additional learning opportunities outside of school, provide intensive tutoring, focus on early childhood learning, extend learning during the summer to prevent learning loss, or focus on improving the education experience. Wings for Kids' answer to this question, called the *Wings*

Way, is to focus on developing emotional intelligence. They define emotional intelligence as the "ability to perceive, control, and evaluate emotions" (www.wingsforkids.org). Using available research enables the organization to connect emotional intelligence directly to their mission of children succeeding in school. According to their website (Wings for Kids, n.d.c), "Social emotional learning addresses children's ability to learn about and manage their emotions and interactions with others—the skills all children need to succeed in school, form healthy relationships, and eventually excel in the workplace."

This adds clarity but it still leaves considerable room for interpretation. What "knowledge, attitudes, and skills" do children need to demonstrate emotional intelligence? Wings for Kids defines five interrelated core competencies that support social emotional learning:

- **Self-awareness.** Understanding emotions and thoughts and how they influence behavior. Skills include self-perception, self-confidence, and self-efficacy.
- **Self-management.** The ability to regulate emotions and behaviors in different situations and to set and work toward goals. Skills include impulse control, executive function, stress management, and self-discipline.
- **Responsible decision-making.** The ability to make positive choices and take responsibility for positive and negative outcomes. Skills include identifying problems, analyzing situations, solving problems, and reflection.
- **Social awareness.** The ability to empathize with others. Skills include empathy, appreciating differences, and respect.
- **Relationship skills.** The ability to relate well to others. Skills include communicating clearly, listening, cooperation, resisting negative pressure, resolving conflicts, and supporting one another.

Their website (Wings for Kids, n.d.b) states "Everything we do at WINGS is rooted in these five core competencies and corresponding skills." Defining a specific outcome and the skills needed to support that outcome provides everyone associated with Wings—staff and board members, volunteers, partners, parents, kids, teachers, and donors—a clear picture of the outcomes·they seek and why they matter. Because their outcomes are grounded in research, they have credibility and validity.

Identify who will be affected. Mission statements often focus on serving a specific group, such as at-risk youth, those who need us most, people facing an emergency, or sometimes a specific geographic area such as a city, county, or neighborhood. Specifying who will benefit provides a compelling case for support. Every organization needs a clear strategy for how they will reach the target population referenced in their mission. This is an area where organizations can experience mission drift. It can be easier and less expensive to serve a population that needs minimal support versus a population that requires extensive support to achieve desired outcomes.

The organization needs to develop a specific definition of who will be affected by their mission and a strategy for how they will identify and reach the desired population. Let's look at how Wings for Kids focuses on their mission to "equip at-risk kids." Wings for Kids defines their target population as children in the US living in poverty. They make the case that child poverty is "associated with a high risk for poor cognitive and academic outcomes, lower school attendance, and grade failure." They cite relevant data to support their case:

- By fourth grade, students living in the poorest families lag academically 12–18 months behind their high-income peers.
- Low-income students are chronically absent at a rate of three to four times higher than other students.
- Low-income students drop out of high school at a rate 4.4 times greater than higher-income students.

Keeping a Mission Focus

When I led a teen program in Philadelphia, we had an ongoing dialogue with our staff about whom we should be serving. Our mission stated we focused on at-risk youth, and in fact the name of the organization was Crime Prevention Association. All youth in the community were invited to participate in our programs, but through partnerships with

> juvenile court, schools, and police we worked hard to reach at-risk youth. These youth were more likely to have behavior challenges when they participated in our programs. We discussed ways of handling specific kids at weekly staff meetings. Staff members frequently questioned if some of these youth should be in our building. We constantly reinforced that although some of these young people were a challenge, they were the kids our mission demanded us to serve. Our discussions focused on how to keep the most challenging teens engaged and the best strategies for helping them to succeed.

Wings for Kids engages at-risk youth by working exclusively in Title 1 elementary schools that predominately serve youth from low-income families. By building a strong foundation of emotional intelligence skills in elementary school, Wings for Kids enables low-income youth "to succeed in school, stay in school, and thrive in life."

In addition to focusing on the quality and impact of the programs and services they provided, many of the leaders I interviewed made growth part of their strategy. The number of people who benefit matters as much as the outcomes the organization achieves because the organization's impact derives from these measures. The challenge for every leader is to find the right balance between how much and how many people can be affected given available resources. A problem occurs when the desire to make a difference leads to overpromising. Your strategy requires an accurate assessment of the resources needed to drive impact for an optimal number of people. If the mission requires a significant investment to make a difference, the strategy needs to reflect this.

Develop a service delivery model that clearly defines what services and programs will be provided. Mission strategy requires developing a service delivery model that provides a clear complete description of the programs and services that will bring about the desired outcomes. A service delivery model is based on sound evidence and relevant research about what works and is informed by the organization's experience and learning. The service delivery model provides all stakeholders with a clear picture of how the organization will achieve outcomes. For staff members it provides clear direction about their role in implementing the model. For leaders it clarifies the training and resources staff members need. For donor-investors the service delivery model clearly identifies what funding is needed for the organization to succeed.

Let's continue to look at Wings for Kids service model. The Wings Way (Wings for Kids, n.d.d) is "grounded in the principles of positive youth development and evidenced-based social emotional learning practices. It weaves social emotional learning throughout the program time." Their approach has three pillars:

- **Program culture.** A safe, healthy place where children feel like they belong. The Wings Way includes specific practices and daily activities that staff members are trained to implement.
- **Adult skills.** Adult staff members are trained to model social emotional behavior with youth and peers.
- **Comprehensive curriculum.** Wings for Kids has developed a comprehensive age-specific curriculum with prescribed daily activities that provide explicit and implicit skill-building opportunities across the five core competencies as part of the daily program.

Each pillar has a specific intentional process and resources for how it is operationalized every day. Implementing the Wings Way is supported through extensive staff training and ongoing coaching and feedback. It provides a road map for how Wings for Kids achieves the outcome of social emotional intelligence.

Build partnerships with other nonprofits and government organizations that target the same population. Nonprofit missions address complex and difficult problems that can rarely be resolved by any single organization. In their book *Partnerships for Health and Human Service Nonprofits: From Collaborations to Mergers* the editors make the point that the "nonprofit world is changing, and the future success of nonprofits will be defined and dominated by strategic alignments and partnerships. Funders at all levels are pushing strategic alliances. Innovation that creates social change and impact requires us to abandon our silos and fears and learn to create new partnerships" (Hansen-Turton et al., 2015, p. 3).

Partnerships bring organizations with complementary missions and skill sets together to coordinate their efforts, increase efficiency, and achieve greater impact. I strongly believe partnerships with government, nonprofit organizations, and businesses working together as one network or system focused on collective impact will define the future. We will explore this deeper in Chapter 6.

Building partnerships requires an intentional strategy. It takes an investment of time, but the right partnerships enable every organization involved to advance mission outcomes. An effective strategy focuses on seeking out the partnerships that will make the biggest differences for your service population. This begins by developing relationships and learning about the goals, strategies, and challenges of other organizations working with the same population. Effective partnerships occur when all involved leaders can do the following:

- Define their mission outcomes with clarity about whom they serve and how they will make a difference.
- Clarify the role each organization will play in realizing long-term outcomes.
- Agree on a process for how they will work together.
- Demonstrate greater impact by working together.

Let's take a look at how Wings for Kids made partnerships with public education a core part of their strategy. Wings provides something extra that complements the schools' goals for students. In addition, because the schools and Wings share the same space, regular communication with teachers enables Wings' staff members to work collaboratively to meet the needs of individual youth.

Following is a high-level summary of the Wings for Kids strategy for a mission-outcomes strategy. Wings has significantly more detail about every item, but a simple document built on the mission statement aids communication, creates alignment, and builds credibility.

Summary of Wings for Kids Mission Strategy

	What Outcomes	Who Is Served	How Outcomes Are Achieved
Mission	Kids succeed in school, stay in school, and thrive in life.	At-risk kids	Equip kids with skills.

	What Outcomes	Who Is Served	How Outcomes Are Achieved
Strategy	Increase social emotional learning by supporting development of • Self-awareness • Self-management • Responsible decision-making • Social-awareness • Relationship skills	Reach low-income students by working in partnership with Title 1 elementary schools that serve youth predominately from low-income families.	The Wings Way is "grounded in the principles of positive youth development and evidenced-based social emotional learning practices." Their approach has three pillars: • A safe, healthy place where children feel like they belong • Adult staff trained to model social emotional behavior • A curriculum with explicit and implicit skill-building opportunities

The Resource Center includes a blank template and a suggested process for beginning to develop your organization's strategy under the heading Strategy Development Process Overview and Questions for Leaders.

It is not enough to have a clear, well-thought-out mission strategy. Success requires a strong organization with the know-how and capability needed to fully implement your strategy for achieving mission. There are three tasks for leaders:

- **Establish efficient and effective operating systems** aligned with the organization's mission strategy and goals.
- **Attract and develop talented people with the passion, know-how, and drive to achieve the mission.**
- **Develop a measurement strategy** that supports learning, drives performance, and quantifies results.

Establish efficient and effective operating systems. To be credible, organizations must be well managed with systems and practices that meet expectations for efficient day-to-day operations. As addressed in Chapter 2, generally many organizations do not have sufficient dedicated resources for finance, HR, technology, strategic planning, and resource development. Yet to compete successfully for resources (especially from government and foundations), organizations must demonstrate competency. This can take a major portion of the CPO's time and energy. One CPO described it this way: "Having systems and process to achieve maximum efficiency makes it possible to spend more time with people and on mission." Leaders have two key tasks.

First, make sure the organization's operating systems are at peak efficiency. Operating mechanisms are the routine processes to coordinate and keep the organization functioning day-to-day and year-to-year. In addition to big tasks such as finance, budgeting, planning, and performance management, operating systems include ongoing tasks such as weekly staff meetings, planning daily activities, and board meetings.

This is an area where board members can play a critical role. Board members bring specialized expertise and provide an unbiased perspective to assess how efficiently and effectively the organization operates. In addition, board members can invite others with specialized expertise into the assessment process. The Resource Center for Truth 2 contains links to assessment tools for major areas of operations under the heading Resources for Board and Staff Members to Assess and Build Systems, Practices, and Policies. While incremental improvements are ongoing, annual board-driven assessments and oversight will provide insights to make significant advancements. The more efficient and effective, the more energy can be put toward mission.

Second, align the operating systems with the organization's overall strategy. Many people see operating systems as a series of must-do routine activities. They fail to connect them to their larger mission and goals. If done right, they have the potential to have a huge impact on the organization. For example, one organization had five goals in their strategic plan. They formed a board committee for each goal. Board agendas were built on the five goals with board members providing updates and leading discussions about next steps. The goals were also the basis for setting agendas for staff meetings. This kept the goals front and center to the organization's ongoing operations. It ensures all staff members, volunteers, donor-investors, and the community understand what is important to the organization.

We will spend more time on aligning operating systems to operations in Chapter 4.

Attract and develop people with the passion, know-how, and drive to achieve the mission. People are the critical ingredient in building an organization able to achieve extraordinary results. The best strategy is useless unless the organization has talented people driven by their belief in the organization's mission and goals. This is essential and cannot be compromised. Transformational leaders need a strategy for hiring and developing people "compulsively driven with an insatiable desire to make a difference" (Collins, 2005, p. 3).

Here is how transformational leaders described their people strategy:

- Who[m] we employ makes all the difference. People are key; we need to hire for the things we can't teach. We look first for people who have a passion for the mission, integrity, and a desire to be a positive role model. We can provide training about how to run the program.
- Having trained skilled staff is one of the organization's key strategies for success.
- The organization is always recruiting staff even when we do not have an opening. We do not wait for people to walk in the door. We are always on the lookout for people who could be on our staff. We keep a running list of people who would be good staff. When an opening occurs, we are ready to recruit good hires.
- We have built a strong staff. To keep them and compete for the best talent, we increased benefits and salary.

- Our goal was for every site to be great, and we believed staff make the difference. We had to hire the right people and provide them with training to succeed.
- Staff training is crucial.
- Surrounding yourself with the right people on the board and in the Club is key. Be picky about who works at the Club. Hire first for the things we can't teach, especially passion for mission, integrity, and desire.
- Leadership needs to have a strong focus on empowering staff, providing training and resources, and communicating confidence that they will do a great job.
- We focus on talent at the administrative level and with our program leaders. Our strategy is to have the best people in full-time positions. The full-time staff then train and develop our part-time staff. Turnover is a challenge with our part-time staff; we are raising salaries to reduce.
- We provided training and implemented quality standards to guide staff development and assess ourselves. From the beginning we focused on doing the basics especially well. Programs start and end on time, staff are prepared, they have needed supplies. This sets the foundation for pushing hard to improve.
- Staff training is the most critical part of our strategy for success. We have a week of training for all staff twice a year at the beginning of summer and beginning of fall, monthly training for our managers, and all staff have an opportunity to participate in regional training conferences. When we set a goal, we must figure out what that means for our staff. For example, when we established a goal to increase teen participation, we scheduled two days of training to prepare staff.

There are three major themes that summarize the people strategy in all of those quotes:

- Recruit and hire the right staff members.
- Train and develop staff members to ensure they are successful.
- Provide competitive compensation, benefits, and policies to all staff members.

In small organizations every position is critical. Organizations need a thoughtful process to bring talented people into the organization. Every vacancy creates a crisis and a sense of urgency. The staff members who remain must carry out their own responsibilities and find a way to fill in for vacant positions.

Working in a nonprofit is not for everyone. Salaries are lower, the hours can be long, and missions are challenging. It can sometimes be difficult to feel you are making a difference. It takes resilience to succeed. But the opportunity to contribute to something important is unique. This is the advantage nonprofits have in recruiting staff. Most people crave being part of something that matters, something that is bigger than ourselves, something that makes a difference. Focusing on what your mission demands is the key to hiring, training, and developing staff members.

Hiring Mistakes

My biggest hiring mistakes occurred when I was in a hurry to fill a position. In one case I ended up having to end the employment of the person I hired after six weeks. This was a disaster for the organization and greatly unfair to the person I hired. I knew in my gut this was the wrong person to hire, but I was in a new position, there were multiple vacancies, and I was desperate for help.

Perhaps the best hiring decision I made was when I twice went through interviews with a group of candidates and decided after each round of interviews, we did not have the right person yet. We opened the position for a third time and were able to hire a person that was a perfect fit and exceptional in every way.

Let's look at Wings for Kids' people strategy. Wings has defined clear outcomes supported by a comprehensive service delivery model. Their success depends heavily on the quality of staff-youth interactions. They need staff members who are able to model and teach social emotional learning. They have a few challenges:

- To succeed they need staff members committed to their mission, driven to make a difference, and able to demonstrate social emotional intelligence.
- They need staff members able to implement a comprehensive program model consistently across multiple sites in different cities.
- Because their program generally is only open a few hours a day, they employ a significant number of part-time staff members. There is competition for hiring quality part-time staff members and turnover can be high.

Wings for Kids' strategy for staffing their program begins by recruiting students between their freshman and sophomore year in college. The students hired have a part-time job for three years with annual increases in wages while gaining valuable experience and training to prepare for their career. For Wings, they hire staff members who identify with their mission with an expectation of staying for the three years.

Before they begin students complete an intense two-week training program. Once on the job they are regularly observed and coached to further develop the skills addressed in the training. Everyone who works at Wings completes a full week of professional development and four shorter training sessions annually. Their part-time staff members provide a pipeline for full-time openings. Many of the full-time positions at Wings are filled by former part-time staff members. Imagine the advantage of being able to fill full-time positions with a proven performer with three years of experience in your program. When Wings expands to new cities, they have a replicable model for staffing their program. Wings for Kids' strategy for hiring part-time and full-time positions is integral to their success.

On-the-Job Orientation and Training

Training does not always need to be a formal event; the best training often takes place on the job. I started my career as a student intern at the South Philadelphia Community Center working in the Teen/Youth Service Program. My direct supervisor was Mike Walker, the assistant center director. Mike told me on my first day that my assignment for the next two weeks was to meet 10 new teens every day. I was to learn their name, grade in school, where they went to school, what they liked to do at the center, and one other interesting fact about them.

I met with Mike at the end of every day to share what I learned. Our discussions always ended with a conversation about the importance of relationships and how I might follow up with the kids I met. This assignment lasted for two weeks. It was easy to meet 10 new teens the first few days, but by the second week I had to seek out the kids who were not as easy to connect with—the ones our mission described as needing us most. I didn't fully appreciate the brilliance of Mike's orientation at the time. It was tied to mission, clearly communicated we achieve our mission by connecting with youth, stressed the focus on kids who needed us the most, and provided direction about how I could make a difference.

Develop a measurement strategy that supports learning, drives performance, and quantifies results. A report commissioned by the Alliance for Strong Families and Communities (2020) states that "members of the human services ecosystem must commit to the achievement and measurement of outcomes in all practices, policies, and regulatory and budget mechanisms. This includes focus on a common set of outcomes rather than services delivered and core measures with accountability, full funding, incentives, disincentives, and flexibility."

Transformational leaders understand that outcome measurement is integral to their success. Measurement enables leaders to accomplish the following goals:

- **Identify how to get better.** This is the most important reason to measure. Nonprofits have an ethical obligation to investors and the people targeted by their mission to maximize the use of available resources to make a difference. It is impossible to determine what is working and identify strategies for making a bigger difference without data.

- **Drive performance and accountability.** Although the saying "What gets measured gets done" has become a cliché, it is an important component of the organization's strategy to focus efforts on what is most important. Information is used to make decisions, assess performance, and improve results. One CPO shared that it takes discipline on their part to make sure everyone is aligned to the organization's mission and goals. Measurement is an important tool. Measurable goals are part of everyone's performance plan.

- **Communicate impact and provide a picture of the value the organization creates** for individuals and the community. Data are needed to demonstrate to donor-investors and other stakeholders that the organization affects important outcomes.

Here are some examples of how board and staff leaders described the need for measuring impact:

- Early on we made a commitment to become a data-driven organization. The result was a more efficient and more impactful program.
- We worked to clearly define our role and what we contribute that no one else is providing. That is what we needed to measure.
- Our data is a strength. Being able to demonstrate our outcomes was the driver behind building a partnership with the school district that fueled our growth.
- We created measurements for the goals in our strategic plan and made them part of everyone's individual goals.

Transformational leaders establish a comprehensive measurement strategy that clearly defines desired outcomes, what information is collected, how it is collected, and how it is used. Transformational leaders develop a measurement strategy with three levels (BGCA, 2006):

Level 1: Participation: Whom do we serve, how many do we serve, and how much service is provided?

Level 2: Assessment: How well are we implementing our service strategy?
Level 3: Outcome measurement: What difference do we make?

Level 1: Participation demonstrates the organization is reaching a significant number of the population described in the mission statement frequently enough to make a difference. Participation is not proof of impact, but it is an important indicator that something positive is happening at a significant scale. Participation information generally answers four basic questions about the organization's performance:

- How many people do we reach?
- Whom do we serve? What number or percentage of the population targeted in our mission statement do we reach?
- How frequently do they participate?
- How long do they stay involved?

Organizational goals for these metrics provide a perspective for assessing performance. This information can also be used to begin telling a compelling story about the difference the organization makes. For example, the Wings for Kids evaluation found that children who at a minimum participated in the program for two years and attended at least 100 days realized the greatest impact. Focusing on how many children stay in the program for at least two years and attend 100 days becomes an indicator of greater impact.

Level 2: Assessment measures how well the organization implements its mission strategy and how effective the organization operates. There are two parts to this:

- First, how efficient, and effective are our operating mechanisms? Do they reflect best practices and standards for nonprofit organizations for functions like financial management, human resources, and board engagement? The Resource Center for Truth 2 contains overviews and links to numerous organizational assessment tools under the heading Resources for Board and Staff Members to Assess and Build Systems, Practices, and Policies.
- Second, how well are we implementing our mission strategy? The mission strategy specifies the programs and services the

organization believes will achieve the desired mission outcomes. Assessing how well actual services reflect relevant
research and evidence-based practices is essential for learning
and developing a plan to increase program effectiveness. For
example, the Wings for Kids study (n.d.e) "showed that the
adult social emotional skills are essential to delivering a program that results in measurable child outcomes." Wings used
this information to strengthen their training and staffing model.
Annual and ongoing assessments of how well the service delivery model is being implemented are important measures of success and opportunities for further learning.

Level 3: Outcome measurement is the most challenging component of
your measurement strategy. Outcome measurement enables leaders to
accomplish the following:

- Demonstrate the efficacy of their services and programs. It is
  nearly impossible to know if the services the organization provides are making a difference without measuring outcomes.
  This is not simply good business; leaders driven by mission are
  obligated to know how well the organization is achieving
  its mission.
- Identify how to increase impact of services and programs. Data-
  driven organizations use outcome data to strengthen all aspects
  of their mission strategy to achieve greater impact.
- Make the case to donors to invest in their organization. People
  want to support organizations that demonstrate and quantify
  the difference they make.

Let's take a look at Wings for Kids' approach to outcome measurement.
As mentioned, in addition to ongoing assessment of impact, Wings for Kids
participated in an RCT. Their efforts enabled Wings for Kids to make a
statement such as this: "The RCT study provides evidence of the positive
impact on academic performance and classroom behavior resulting from
the explicit teaching of social emotional skills to at-risk students during
afterschool hours."

Their evaluation also enables Wings for Kids to develop a comprehensive strategy for how they can further increase their impact by assessing

the information, identify learning, and strengthening the program. For example, the evaluation found that staff ability to support social emotional learning was dependent on staff ability to role-model positive social emotional behavior. WINGS already provided training to staff members to help them understand their social emotional skills, but the finding enabled them to further strengthen their efforts.

Most organizations will not be able to afford a comprehensive third-party evaluation. But every organization needs a measurement strategy focused on how well they are achieving their mission. Too often organizations measure outcomes primarily to satisfy funding requirements. This makes the whole effort a colossal waste of time. Transformational leaders believe measurement is key to organizational learning that drives impact. They invite all stakeholders to be part of the learning process. They discuss the results openly and regularly to identify learning, continue to strengthen their service model, and communicate about impact.

Examining the information the organization collects can lead to many possible conclusions. Each scenario leads to an opportunity for learning and adjustments to enhance results. For example:

- If results are below expectations, but the service model is not being fully implemented, the focus then is on more rigorous implementation of the service strategy. This may involve staff training, reallocation of resources, or more ongoing support to staff.
- If results are below expectations, and the service model is being implemented, the focus then is on adjusting the service model. One approach might be looking at when and where you are getting the best results.
- If results are good, but the service model is not being implemented, it requires an assessment of what is being done and determining why and how the service model was abandoned. A revision to the service model may be required to reflect learning about why the organization is getting good results.
- If results are good, and the service model is being implemented, it does not mean efforts shouldn't be put toward improving results. For example, if the organization provides services at multiple locations, looking at the locations that achieve the best results can lead to insights about how to enhance services. Boys & Girls Clubs of America looked at outcome results from

the Club sites that were in the 90th percentile in terms of results to identify staff members and organizational practices that made the biggest difference.

- Results are good, but very few people are participating. Regardless of the results, how often people participate and how long they engaged is important. Leaders should ask, Are there others who could benefit and are not being reached? How can the organization increase reach? Can it be done with the same resources or are additional resources needed. Being able to quantify the difference additional resources will make can be a powerful support to resource development.

There are many excellent resources to support developing a comprehensive measurement strategy in the Resource Center beginning with a step-by-step guide under the heading Developing and Implementing an Outcome Measurement Strategy. The Resource Center also contains information and links to additional resources to support specific components of your measurement plan.

Let's check to see how Helen is doing with implementing her measurement strategy.

Community Centers of Mission City Measurement Plan

Helen tasked Daniel, the new director of operations, to begin developing the Center's measurement strategy. Currently the only data they had was a daily participation log and program enrollment. Because providing a safe nurturing environment was a priority, they decided they would begin by measuring how parents viewed the safety of their children at the centers. They developed a short survey parents could answer in a few minutes. Parents were asked as they entered the building over a two-week period to complete the survey. Graduate students would administer the survey and compile the results.

Some of the staff members, including Hazel, the center director at the West Side Community Center, were strongly opposed to the plan. When the students began asking parents to complete the survey

Hazel advised parents that it was not important and encouraged them to say they didn't have time today. After Helen and Daniel intervened Hazel relented but didn't hesitate to let everyone know she felt it was a waste of time.

The results of the safety assessment were not as positive as everyone expected them to be. Everyone was sure parents believed their children were safe at the center. Of the surveyed parents 25% indicated their children did not always feel safe at the center; only about 30% reported that their children always feel safe and 45% felt safe most of the time. Staff members were surprised by this result. Many believed the results were not true. They said, "The survey was poorly worded." "The students didn't record the data accurately." "The whole idea of measurement is a waste of time, and this proved it." Hazel was the most outspoken. "I don't need a survey to tell us our children feel safe."

After much discussion Daniel recognized the concerns. "I know these are not the results we hoped for, but we cannot abandon our efforts. It would be wrong to ignore these findings. We need to understand better what is going on and figure out how to improve results. We need a plan for how we can have follow-up conversations with some of the parents and some of the older children to better understand when they feel safe and when they do not."

After the meeting Hazel followed Daniel to his office and closed the door. "I am not going to ask any of our parents or kids to be part of some focus group. The West Side Community Center will not participate in the focus group." Daniel tried unsuccessfully to understand Hazel's concerns and change her point of view. She left repeating, "do not plan any follow-up at the West Side Center."

Daniel shared Hazel's views with Helen. They determined they would have one more conversation with Hazel about the importance of not just participating but supporting the organization's measurement efforts. They would emphasize how her experience and insight would be an asset to identifying the underlying problem. If she did not pledge cooperation, they would put their concerns in writing. Helen alerted board chair Hank Salvan and HR committee chair Leslie Silver about the challenge.

How should Helen respond if Hazel does not embrace the measurement initiative? What would you do?

Measurement Resistance

New measurement initiatives often are met with resistance. I experienced this early in my career. As part of a graduate school field placement, I was asked to evaluate the effectiveness of a court diversion program for juvenile offenders. The agency I was place with worked with first-time youth offenders over a period of three to six months. If they stayed out of trouble the charges against them would be dismissed. The key was intensive case work during that time. We had three centers and were serving about 100 youth at each center. I read through every file, including all the notes our youth counselors made about each youth for the previous three years. Nearly all youth in the program were not getting arrested again, but one key finding was that on average youth stayed in the program for 19 months. Our proposal and our literature were clear—this was an intensive three- to six-month intervention that got kids back on track.

When the CPO read my report, he called me to his office to tell me I was wrong—that was not how the program worked. I held my ground and eventually convinced him my data were correct. When I presented the findings to the staff members the reaction was even stronger. The initial reaction was it wasn't true. When they became convinced it was true, they believed the program model should be changed to keep youth in the program longer to make a difference. Eventually we were able to clarify goals and revise the program model. We initiated a process for staff members to formally review continued participation in the program at the end of six months. This included the development of a plan to transition them out of the diversion program but remain active in our teen program.

New measurement initiatives often meet with resistance. Several of the CPOs interviewed described having to let staff members go because they refused to embrace the measurement strategy. They created a measurement system and provided staff members with training but this was a big cultural shift and they experienced considerable resistance. They needed everyone to be committed to the measurement strategy. In the end some staff members were asked to leave, and some left on their own.

Resistance comes in two ways. The first is not taking the time to collect accurate, timely data. The argument is that collecting data takes time away from program. Although this might be true initially, once data collection is part of the daily routine it becomes how the work is done, not something extra to do. The second form of resistance occurs when the data are presented. Measurement initiatives are generally a mix of good results and opportunities to improve. The reaction to opportunities to improve is often, "there is something wrong with the way we measured." Or, "I knew this instrument did not ask the right questions." Or, "I knew this was a waste of time, I know we are doing better than this."

Organizations need resources to pursue their mission. Every nonprofit leader wakes up in the morning asking, "Where will we find the resources our organization needs to thrive and deliver on the promise of our mission?" Most of the organizations I examined were struggling financially when the CPO who transformed the organization was hired. Income had stagnated or declined, meeting payroll was frequently a challenge, and there were few resources for new ventures. Yet every organization I examined more than doubled their annual operating revenue over a five-year period, some even tripled and quadrupled their revenue (overall nonprofit revenue grew about 4% annually during this same period). Though resources were an issue when the leader began, a new resource development strategy was not their initial focus. So, what was the secret to their success?

First, mission was the foundation of the organization's resource development strategy. The missions of nonprofit organizations represent the best of our collective values and beliefs. They are critical to the future strength of every community. Transformational leaders—board members and professionals—share a fanatical belief in the importance of their mission. A strong belief in mission is contagious. Transformational leaders inspire others to make investing in the organization's mission a priority. But belief in mission is only a starting point; it is not enough by itself.

Second, the organization demonstrated it is efficient and well managed. As indicated in Truth 2, transformational leaders fixed, stabilized, or replaced systems, practices, and people who were not working. When an organization does not operate effectively, leaders must spend most of their time in a reactive mode—solving problems, sorting through chaos, and providing direction to every decision. There is little time to move the organization forward. Transformational leaders demonstrate through actions that the organization aspires to excellence in every aspect of operations. They ensure existing funding is stable by beginning to share their vision and goals for the organization and sharing the steps they are taking to strengthen the organization. They seek advice and input. In some cases, key donor-investors can play a critical role in encouraging and supporting needed organizational changes especially when a new CPO is being hired. Donor-investors may believe in the importance of the organization's mission, but they want to make sure their investment will make a difference.

Third, to grow resources, leaders demonstrated how increased revenue will result in increased reach and greater impact. Transformational leaders establish a clear strategy that defines mission outcomes and describes how the organization will achieve and measure outcomes. Demonstrating a commitment to outcome measurement is critical. People want to invest in organizations that get results. In my experience, if you don't have a plan to define and measure outcomes your donor-investors are likely to establish one for you. Their plan may be based on their needs not the organization's.

In short, transformational leaders recognize that the foundation for a successful resource development strategy comprises the following components:

- A fanatic belief and commitment to mission by board and staff members that is inspiring and draws others to the organization
- Building a reputation as an organization that meets high operational standards and aspires to excellence in everything they do
- Articulating mission outcomes and a clear strategy for how the organization pursues its mission; the strategy is easy to understand, informed by evidence, and comprehensive enough to be credible
- Gathering evidence to demonstrate results and learn how to get better results

Leaders—staff and board members—weave this information into a compelling story that inspires, excites, and builds confidence. These are the ingredients needed to engage donor-investors (Grace, 2005) in a mission-focused partnership. Many of the leaders described an upward spiral of increased resources. As the organization became more effective, trust and awareness increased, followed by new opportunities to acquire resources. More resources provide the fuel to increase scale and impact. This leads to increased visibility and sets the stage for further growing resources. Here are some examples of how CPOs described their resource development success:

- We focused on building awareness about a strong, clear mission and raising dollars to support this.
- We started by raising the profile of the organization as well managed and effective.
- As we began to grow, awareness and support increased.
- I believed our program had to be exemplary for the organization to succeed. This was first and foremost about our mission but focus on quality programs enabled us to achieve a high profile in the community and ultimately to raising more money.
- As we grew and operated more effectively, we began to have a seat at the table.

Several leaders shared how strengthening operations and building a clear mission-driven strategy led to increased awareness. Increased awareness is dependent on the public's perception of the importance of the organization's mission and desired outcomes, and the organization's capacity to demonstrate they can make a difference. Awareness and a positive reputation grow as organizations articulate and validate results. Awareness of the organization's viability lifts its profile. This becomes an upward spiral. Increased belief in capacity to achieve an important mission leads to increased resources, which leads to more increases in mission outcomes and additional resources. Transformational leaders continue to share the organization's mission, vision, and impact.

Initially many organizations depended on government and foundations grants supplemented by income from special events. To grow operating revenue, nearly all the organizations determined at some point they must expand income from individuals. Individual giving generally is counted as operating revenue that can be allocated at the board's discretion, whereas a most grants are restricted to spending for a specific project or purpose.

These organizations were remarkably successful at growing revenue from individual giving. Following are examples of how CPOs and board members framed and carried out this strategy. Note the emphasis on setting a goal and keeping it in the forefront. Without a clear goal, organizations are stuck doing business the same year after year. We will discuss the importance of this practice in more detail in Chapter 4.

- Early on, event income drove increases in revenue. Then we began a campaign to increase individual giving.
- Our resource development was focused on events. There was no organizational process for determining how these would be planned and executed. We started by creating a calendar and clarifying roles.
- We needed to diversify revenue; we were almost totally grant-driven. We set goals for new revenue from individuals and corporations and reported progress at every board meeting. Most of our recent revenue growth has been from individuals.

- We needed to engage high-wealth donors to build individual giving. Our focus now is on increasing individual and corporate giving. We keep it in front of the organization by reporting progress on our goals and discussing next steps at every board meeting.
- We had an endowment discussion early on in my tenure. The board voted to have a $10 million dollar endowment. We asked what will happen if we do not build an endowment? We set a big goal to have an $8 million endowment within three years. We put this in writing and said it out loud. We were probably naive, but our commitment gave us focus. Every campaign we did for a new facility included a goal of five years of operating expenses.
- We grew from 6 major gifts in 2012 to 170 major gifts in 2015. Now 70% of our budget comes from individual gifts.
- Our resource development strategy is relationships.
- Our board worked shoulder-to-shoulder with staff on fund raising. We gave personally and opened many doors to new donors.
- We are now focused on building an endowment. We set a goal of having a $40 million endowment.

Note how these examples highlight the important role of board members in resource development. Adding significant new revenue must be driven by the CPO and board members working in partnership. People invest in people as much as in mission. This is true for the board and staff leaders. Board members must be actively engaged in resource development. To grow revenue from individuals, board members must open doors and invite others to support the organization.

In summary, a well-thought-out, mission-driven strategy prepares transformational leaders to engage potential donor-investors in an ongoing conversation to find where they can fit into your mission-outcomes strategy. This requires a thoughtful strategy based on research and learning and taking the time to build relationships to discover what is important to each donor. This is the key to raising operating dollars (Grace, 2005).

Operating Versus Restricted Funding

Every organization I ever worked for struggled at times with raising operating versus restricted funding. Restricted funds can only be used for a specific project. Too often organizations compromise and accept grants that require them to implement a program or service that is not central to their mission-driven strategy. Their budget grows, but some of that growth may be a distraction from their mission strategy. Pressure on mission from grants that don't quite fit can lead to mission creep. Having a clear strategy that defines outcomes and how they will be achieved provides an opportunity to engage funders in a conversation about supporting your core mission.

One final thought about resource development. If you Google fund raising or resource development, you will find many sites that have multiple ideas for increasing revenue. This is great, you need ideas to engage potential donor-investors. But without staff and board members who are fanatical about mission, without an efficient organization implementing a clear strategy for success, and without leaders willing and able to engage people in a conversation about the importance of the difference the organization makes—all the great ideas in the world will not lead to sustainable growth in the organization's capacity to acquire resources that drive mission.

The Resource Center contains information called Resource Development Resources about where to locate information and many excellent tools to support your resource development strategy.

Let's check in to see how Helen and the Community Centers of Mission City are doing with their strategy.

Community Centers of Mission City Board Meeting One Month After Board Retreat

Board chair Hank Salvan called the meeting to order. "Since our last meeting, the strategic planning committee and Helen have met several times. They have interviewed community leaders, government officials, and other nonprofits in Mission City. I am going to ask Frances Stillman, chair of the strategic planning committee, to provide us with an overview."

"We used the strategy model from the book The Five Truths for Transformational Leaders *to guide our work. There are three components to this model:*

- *Mission outcomes. What outcomes will we deliver and to whom?*
- *Organizational capability. What will our organization need to be exceptionally good at to drive our outcomes? How will we know if we are succeeding?*
- *Resources acquisition. How will we build awareness and acquire the resources needed to deliver superior performance relative to our mission outcomes?*

You received a summary of our draft strategy with the agenda for this meeting. Before I walk you through the handout, let me say that our strategy, simply put, is to support families in the communities we serve. We will provide some services directly, but we will also work with other nonprofits and government agencies to make support families need to thrive easy to access.

Community Centers of Mission City Strategy Overview

Our goal is to triple the number of individuals and families we reach in five years by working in partnership with other nonprofits and government agencies to make critical lifesaving services easily available in the community.

Community Centers of Mission City Mission Strategy

	Outcomes	Who	How
Mission	Families that thrive	Children and families in underserved communities	Work collaboratively to provide access to programs and resources to empower them to thrive
Strategy	Children and families feel safe, welcomed, and connected in our building. Families live healthy lifestyles and make healthy choices. Children achieve positive physical, educational, and emotional milestones.	Location in areas with a high percentage of families living at or below poverty level. Increase outreach to other organizations in the community to coordinate service and make it easy for families to a access services.	All families have access to basic needs-food, shelter and health care. Provide essential services in our communities in a safe welcoming environment. Priority services include: • Pre-school and after-school childcare • Meal Programs • Recreation and educational programs for family members • Family Counseling • Health Programs: Access to health care and information to support healthy lifestyles

Organizational capability. *Partnerships are the key to our strategy. Currently we operate a preschool, but after-school childcare is provided in our buildings by the Mission City Boys & Girls Club. Our community health clinic is operated by the Mission City Hospital. We will need to strengthen and expand these relationships and build new partnerships. Our goal is to bring more services to the community. We will need staff members exceptionally good at developing strong relationships and working collaboratively with other organizations.*

Measuring outcomes will be an important component of our strategy. To know if we are making a difference, increasing impact, and attracting resources we need a comprehensive measurement strategy. Our measurement strategy must accurately track how many people we reach, assess organizational effectiveness, and measure outcomes for the people and families in our program. As safety is core to our success, we will begin measuring how safe children and families feel in our centers.

Resource acquisition. *To fully implement our strategy, we will need additional resources. Although we will continue to apply for grants that fit our strategy, we will shift our development focus to growing individual and corporate support to provide the operating revenue needed to support our mission.*

We are going to need to make a substantial investment to upgrade our facilities. However, the strategic planning committee believes we need to operationalize our strategy and enhance our reputation before undertaking a capital campaign. Through a grant from the Community Foundation and the work of many volunteers, we have patched up our buildings.

The strategy presentation was followed by an enthusiastic discussion with many questions and ideas for strengthening the strategy. Hank closed the meeting by asking Frances and the strategic planning committee to work with Helen to make adjustments based on the board's feedback. "I also believe we need a plan for the next 12 to 18 months with specific goals and an outline of the steps we must take to realize our goals. We have considerable work to do to align staff, partners, and donors on our strategy. The final six months of this plan should include development of a strategic plan and exploration of a capital campaign to repair or replace our facilities and increase our operating revenue. This will require the board to be more involved in resource development." A few board members raised concerns about what "being more involved in resource development" means, but Hank indicated they would discuss this as part of the ongoing planning process.

Over the next month Helen met with important stakeholders including funders, staff and board members, and community leaders to share the draft strategy and seek feedback. The feedback was incredibly positive and helpful. The strategic planning committee was prepared to present an overview of the final strategy at the next board meeting.

Hank again shared with Helen the need for her to begin changing what she focuses on. "You have done an admirable job of getting the organization on a good path. Continuing to grow the organization will require a new focus. The work you have done to engage stakeholders is a good example of how you will need to focus more of your energy."

Helen remained confused about what exactly this meant. What advice do you have for Helen?

Summary

Nonprofit organizations that are poised to grow and prosper (to be transformed) focus on the following actions:

- Have an important mission that leaders translate into action
- Are well-managed by strong transformational board and staff leaders
- Have a sound strategy for how they will achieve the mission
- Measure results to demonstrate impact and discover opportunities to increase impact
- Are able to acquire resources to drive growth and impact

Strategy makes the case for why your mission is important and how the community will be better because of the work of your organization. The best strategy is simple on the surface; it can be explained in a few sentences. It is also well thought out with complexity built vertically. It is captured on paper and used to train staff members, share with the public, or to put into a proposal.

Developing the organization's strategy is not a one-time event. Strategy is continuously updated and upgraded through an ongoing process of providing services, assessing results, identifying learning, and implementing improvements, combined with a quest for superior knowledge of the research and learning related to your mission. Transformational leaders take advantage of every opportunity to engage all stakeholders—staff and board members, donors, community leaders—through ongoing conversations about how the organization makes a difference and how it can become even stronger.

An organization's strategy must address all three components of a mission-driven strategy:

- If the organization cannot convince people their mission outcomes are important, it will be difficult to attract resources no matter how well thought out their strategy to achieve the mission or how skilled they are at resource development.
- If mission outcomes are deemed important but the organization cannot demonstrate the capacity to achieve the outcomes it will be difficult to continue to attract resources.
- If the organization has a clear mission and capacity to achieve outcomes but is unable to identify investors willing to provide operating resources, the organization will fail.

Having the right strategy is essential but the organization must be able to successfully execute the strategy to be successful. Transformational leaders align the entire organization behind the strategy. Successfully executing the strategy requires exceptional clarity about goals and the role of every stakeholder in achieving the goals. This is the focus of Truth 4 in the next chapter.

Notes for Board Members

An ongoing discussion of a mission-driven strategy is key to the success of nonprofit organizations. Strategy development is the most important work the board does. This seems simple and obvious, but many organizations struggle to make this discussion central to the work of the board. Strategy development is not something that occurs once every five years or even once a year. It is an ongoing dynamic process built into every conversation and every meeting. Here is how a few board members described this process:

- The CPO and the board must be able to look backward and look forward at the same time. Together board and staff leaders continuously review where we have been, determine where we want to go, and define how we will get there.
- We need to understand where the organization has been and what is needed to exceed now and five years in the future. We need to take stock of what the leader will need to do to succeed now and in the future.
- The focus of our organization is continuously updated based on learning, experience, and evolving conditions in the operating environment.

To succeed, board and staff leaders need a strategy for ongoing board development and for planning effective meetings.

Board development is an important part of the CPO's role. Working in partnership with board leaders, the goal is to build an influential board that is able to govern, establish strategy, and ensure the organization has necessary resources to achieve its mission. I asked board and professional leaders to describe their strategy and philosophy for board development. Four themes emerged:

- **Build strong relationships.** Every CPO indicated they made a concerted effort to talk with every board member one-to-one on a regular basis. These were not social visits; the CPO took the opportunity to share the organization's challenges and successes and asked for the board member's advice. This is also an important opportunity to involve board members in strategic discussions. The Resource Center contains a list of suggested questions for CPOs to help start the discussion under the heading in Truth 1 for CPO Guide to Building Relationships Conversation Starters. Here is how some board members framed the importance of relationship building:

  - Our CPO develops personal relationships with each board member. He is good at engaging in a way that makes every board member valuable to the organization.

- She continues to build relationships, meets each member where they are, and plugs them in where they can succeed. Nobody does this better than her.
- The CPO must have strong communication skills. The CPO's role is to organize communication to the board to enable them to see the organization's impact.
- Board members need opportunities to get to know each other informally. We have informal time before or after our board meetings.
- Our CPO gets to know each board member and takes the time to understand their passions and background. Relationships are deep and genuine.

- **Role clarity is essential.** To be effective, board members need to know what is expected of them. This should be captured in job descriptions and annual goals for each board member. The board's primary roles are strategy, governance, resource development, and supervising the CPO. The CPO and other staff members are responsible for implementing strategy. The board needs to trust and empower the CPO to carry out the organization's strategy. Here is some advice from board members:

  - Be intentional about what the board needs to do. Be extremely specific. Board members need to know how they can help.
  - Our CPO coaches each board member about the contribution they can make to the organization.
  - The board has to trust the CPO to deal with the everyday operations of the organization. Our role is in strategy, not operations.
  - Our CPO has relationships with board members that are deep and genuine. He gets to know each board member. He takes time to understand their passions and background. Nobody does this better than [he does]. He coaches each board member to make a unique contribution to the organization. He is very strategic about identifying the right people. He asks, who are the people in the community who can help us realize the goals in our strategic plan?

- Clarify the board's role in resource development. This is an area where many organizations struggle. It is difficult to build a comprehensive resource development strategy without active board engagement. John Carver, the author of numerous books on nonprofit boards, believes that boards must make a formal decision to be actively engaged in fundraising (Carver, 2006). Carver shared this view during a session at a Boys & Girls Clubs of America National Conference in the early 2000s. There was a strong reaction from the Boys & Girls Club leaders in attendance. They believed it was not a choice but a responsibility of the board to support resource development. There is a point on both sides. Boards are essential to implementing a comprehensive fundraising strategy especially for individual giving. However, in many organizations the CPO often complains that the board is not as supportive and as engaged in resource development as they need to be. This becomes a source of ongoing tension between the staff and board members that never gets fully resolved. A board-to-board discussion is required to clarify the board's role in resource development. Organizations with board members actively engaged in resource development have adopted specific expectations with annual goals for the organization and each board member. As Carver suggests, these boards have made a conscious decision about their role in resource development. Here is how board members described their role in resource development:

  - The board needs to feel responsible for resource development. We are blessed to have a board member who is a relentless fundraiser. He motivates everyone to do their part.
  - We have a resource development focused training at our board meetings.
  - Everyone is enthusiastic, and all are willing to give time and money.

- The board worked shoulder-to-shoulder with staff on fund raising. They gave personally and opened many doors to other donors.

- **Continue focus on board recruitment and development.** As organizations grow and evolve the board must change and evolve with the organization. We will address this in more detail when we get to the Truth 5: Continue to Grow as a Leader. Generally, changes to board makeup occur gradually. The CPO working closely with board leaders must address this continuously. Following is advice from CPOs and board leaders.

  - Some board members left—we put term limits in place to help this happen. We were very strategic about recruiting new board members. We needed to get the right people on the board.
  - Only 4 board members out of 14 showed up for my first board meeting. Two years later we had 14 active board members with only 1 remaining from the original board.
  - It is an ongoing priority to evolve the board roster.
  - Initially we had a grassroots board, mostly people with big hearts that wanted this for the community. As we grew, the board transitioned gradually to a board with broad influence. We were very strategic about identifying the right people. We asked, who are the people in the community who can help us realize the goals in our strategic plan?
  - When recruiting for board be very mindful of what the board needs; don't settle.
  - Recruit a high-caliber board of community leaders. You need the people the community will recognize as leaders and influencers.
  - We have board members with different backgrounds and expertise. The board is made up of diverse people, [and] each brings something unique to the organization.

Effective board meetings. Engaging board meetings that feature consequential discussions of the most significant challenges facing the organization are critical to the health and strength of the organization. These consequential discussions are the reason people join boards. To identify the ingredients of an effective board meeting, I asked every CPO and every board member I interviewed to describe the best board meeting they ever attended. Many board members shared that the best board meetings are when the board has a discussion about meaningful questions facing the organization. They also suggested that the worst board meetings are dominated by staff presentations using thick PowerPoint decks filled with information in print too small to read. The CPO and other staff members presenting to the board have to find the right level of detail and leave time for discussion.

Four general themes for planning effective board meetings emerged:

- **Plan meetings that engage board members in important discussions and decisions.** A good meeting starts with the agenda and meeting plan. The key is to figure out what questions to ask. The discussion questions should appear in the agenda to enable board members to come prepared. One board member shared that "our CPO is strategic in planning each meeting. He thinks through what the organization needs from the board and plans the meeting accordingly. He is able to narrow down from amorphous and open-ended questions to something specific that the board can contribute." Another board chair shared that she and the CPO completed an annual plan for their board meeting agendas. The plan may change based on circumstances, but the annual plan helped them to focus on the big picture. Board members offered this advice about planning board meetings:

  - Board meetings must have a purpose. This is a decision-making body; we need a thoughtful process for discussion and decision-making.
  - The best board meeting was when we made a decision tied to our strategic plan to "grow deeper not wider." We made a commitment to serve 100 kids who were on the waiting list.

After we made the decision, we celebrated the role of everyone—staff and board—who made this decision possible.

- The best board meeting was when we discussed our merger with another organization. We needed to have a productive, vigorous discussion to make the right decision. The decision was not just yes or no, but what we would have to do to make the merger successful and how the organization and the board would need to change.

- Never have a meeting that people would be comfortable missing. You must take full advantage of the opportunity to engage the board in meaningful discussions. Always have one item on the agenda that requires discussion and everyone's input.

- **Plan for board-to-board discussion.** Several board members felt the best meetings were when board members made the presentation and led the discussion. This does two things: the board members work hard to master the material and board members feel comfortable asking questions of other board members. Here are few of the remarks:

  - The best meetings are when we hear from board members—when they do most of the talking.

  - There were five priorities in our strategic plan. Each priority became a board committee. Board members report progress, discuss challenges, and identify opportunities at every meeting.

  - Last year was the first time the finance committee chair presented the budget. There were many questions and good discussion that carried over into the rest of the meeting. Preparing the finance committee to present enabled the information shared to be at the right level for the board as opposed to staff members providing too many details. Many board members said this was the first time they understood the budget.

- Plan for more generative questions at board meetings.
- We always have a generative question on the board agenda that the board is asked to consider in advance and come prepared to discuss. This discussion is the best part of the meeting.

- **Celebrate success.** Celebration highlights what is working and provides an opportunity to recognize specific contributions. Celebration builds confidence, rewards hard work, and motivates people to meet new challenges.

  - The best meetings are when we take time to celebrate a successful year.
  - When we completed our strategic plan, it was the culmination of considerable work. We were excited and celebrated setting some big goals.
  - Connect celebration to the work of the board. Let them know how their input makes a difference.

- **Connect to the mission.** Every board meeting should include a mission moment. It may be sharing a story, inviting someone to speak who benefited from the organization's services, or providing information for discussion that builds understanding about the importance of the organization's mission.

  - The best board meetings have a healthy dose of mission. Mission focus anchors the rest of the meeting in why the board is there. It grounds the board in mission when making important decisions.
  - Every August we have a short meeting and then all the board members get on a bus and go to one of our clubs to work directly with kids. This really energizes the board. The next board meeting is always one of the best of the year.

Resource Center for Truth 3

The following resources are available in the Resource Center at the end of the book and online:

- Strategy Development Worksheet
- Strategy Development Process Overview and Questions for Leaders
- Strategy Development Process
- Developing and Implementing an Outcome Measurement Strategy
- Resources to Support Developing a Logic Model
- Recommended Reading About Measurement
- Logic Model Template
- Resources to Guide Selecting Indicators
- Guidelines for Collecting Accurate Data
- Resource Development Resources

4

Truth 4: Execution Drives Results

"Strategy is a commodity; execution is an art. Leadership is defined by results not attributes."

Peter Drucker

Strategy is useless unless it can be executed. A bold vision, big goals, and a thoughtful strategy mean nothing unless leaders can turn the words into actions that produce meaningful and measurable results. The work you have done so far to implement the first three truths is the foundation for building an efficient, well-managed, high-performance organization with a mission-driven strategy. Transformational leaders work relentlessly to create clarity across the organization about how to execute the strategy. They ensure everyone—staff and board members, donor-investors, and other stakeholders—have clarity about how the organization will execute its mission-driven strategy. To achieve extraordinary results, stakeholders must be aligned on strategy and understand their role in executing the strategy.

Let's take a moment to review what we have discussed so far.

The first truth—Be Fanatical About Mission—focuses on the importance of a fanatical belief in the mission. Mission is why nonprofit organizations exist; it is the basis for every decision big and small. Passion about the mission is the foundation for success, but by itself it does not ensure success. There are many people passionate about mission who fail as leaders.

101

The second truth—Fix, Stabilize, or Replace Systems, Practices, and People Who Are Not Working—requires leaders to confront the challenges the organization faces and make changes. Transformational leaders establish systems, standards, process, and practices that govern day-to-day operations and ensure the organization operates with optimal efficiency. This includes ensuring the organization has the right people. Transformational leaders establish and communicate expectations for staff performance and behavior. Staff members must meet the organization's standards and expectations. Every CPO I interviewed emphasized the importance of having the right people on the board and in the organization. Leaders hire first for the things that we can't teach: passion, integrity and desire. Then experience and skills.

The third truth—Establish a Mission-Driven Strategy—provides a road map for establishing a strategy that defines measurable outcomes, clarifies how the organization will achieve the outcomes, and guides how it will acquire the resources to succeed. It is impossible to create alignment, build energy, and achieve consistent results without a strategy for how the organization will pursue its mission. Every organization needs a clear vision and strategy. The challenge for leaders is to get everyone on the same page and drive results.

Each truth builds on the one before it:

- Nonprofit leaders must be fanatical about mission. Every decision made throughout the organization is made to advance the mission. A fanatical belief in mission enables leaders to inspire others, make difficult decisions, and set high standards of excellence.
- The second truth requires leaders to build an efficient, well-run organization. Transformational leaders initiate changes in people, systems, and processes almost immediately. These changes will likely cause tension and some people may leave the organization. Ultimately implementing the second truth provides leaders with the space to focus more on strategy.
- The third truth enables leaders to articulate a clear answer to key questions about how the organization will deliver on their mission statement. Who will we serve, what difference will we make? How will make a difference?

Strategy is not an end unto itself. It is of little value unless it can be implemented. Too often organizations develop winning strategies or strategic plans that are celebrated, marched out with great fanfare, and then left to gather dust in the storeroom while the organization continues to operate as it always did. This is tragic!

In *Good to Great*, Collins (2001) introduces the Hedgehog Concept. "The essence of a Hedgehog Concept is to attain piercing clarity about how to produce the best long-term results, and then exercising relentless discipline to say, 'No thank you' to opportunities that fail the hedgehog test" (Collins, 2001). The work you did to establish a mission-driven strategy, is your hedgehog concept. The challenge is to stay focused on and execute that strategy.

How do transformational leaders move from words that describe a strategy to fully implementing that strategy and producing meaningful results? Execution is where many leaders fail. They fail because they are unable to turn strategy into action. They fail because they get distracted by the myriad day-to-day challenges and opportunities that demand attention. They fail because staff and board members never understand the role each person must play for the organization to succeed. Although all staff and board members will play key roles, the CPO must lead strategy execution. Here is how staff and board members described the importance of execution:

- Execution requires clarity and universal understanding about the organization's strategy and the discipline to stay focused on what will make the biggest difference.
- It is super easy to get distracted. It takes discipline on my part to stay focused on goals and make sure everyone is aligned around our goals.
- Strategy is too often forgotten once it is created. The CPO must be instrumental in driving the message. Our CPO keeps it alive every day. He communicates strategy and holds everyone to it.
- The difference between successful leaders and those who struggle is the level of commitment to execution. It is easy to create a strategy; it is hard to execute the strategy.

Let's check in to see how Helen and the Community Centers of Mission City are executing their strategy.

Community Center of Mission City One Year Later

Helen's first year as CPO was very busy and at times hectic. But she survived the whirlwind of activity and the many challenges that needed to be addressed. In the beginning everyday presented new challenges. There were problems to solve, financial crises, and many changes to make. She persevered and the Community Centers of Mission City made significant advances. They increased participation, engaged new partners to support health care for children, and reinvigorated some of their long-time partnerships. Helen made safety and providing a safe welcoming environment a priority. It was rewarding to reflect on how far the organization came in the past year.

Board chair Hank Salvan will end his tenure as board chair after the next board meeting. Hank is preparing remarks for his last board meeting as chairperson. He has asked Helen to take him on a tour of the two buildings they operate to discuss the progress they have made and what is next. Hank has taken every opportunity during the last few months to talk with Helen about how her role as leader needs to change and evolve now that the organization has been stabilized. He has been telling her that stabilization is not the goal. A longer term vision and aspirational goals are needed if she is going to take the organization to the next level. Helen continues to be confused by what this means.

As they go through the building Helen points out improvements they have made and the renovations and repairs they still need to make and how each is related to safety. She also talks enthusiastically about the partnerships they have developed that are making health care for children and families accessible. When they enter a preschool room for four-year-olds there is only one staff member in the room with 14 children. That staff person is talking on the phone looking out the window with their back to the room. While that is happening one of the children stands on top of a table and challenges the others to a contest to see how far they can jump while standing on the table.

Another child briefly leaves the room unnoticed. Helen is horrified. She brings the child back in the room and intervenes to redefine the jumping contest. When the staff person finishes her phone call, and another staff person returns to the room, Helen and Hank leave.

Helen profusely apologizes to Hank. "That is not the attention to safety we need to embrace."

Hank asks, "Do you believe the staff members have the same understanding and expectation about what a safe environment looks like as you do?"

Before Helen can answer she notices the floor by the drinking fountain is wet. She excuses herself and retrieves a mop to wipe up the floor. The Center director came by to take over after another staff person informed him that Helen was mopping the floor under the watchful eye of the board chair.

Helen was furious. She informed the Center director she would talk with him later. Hank suggested they find a place to have a cup of coffee and talk about the visit.

Hank began, "I know you are upset, but this is the perfect opportunity to talk about how your role as leader can evolve. You have spent the past year fixing and stabilizing the organization and in the last few months you have defined a clear strategy for how the organization will make a bigger difference. Grounding everything in the pursuit of safety was brilliant; no one can dispute the need to keep children and families safe. Now everyone in the organization must fully embrace and understand the strategy as deeply as you. More important, they need to know what it means for them. By everyone I mean everyone board and staff members, donor-investors, partners, and community leaders. You can't be the only one to have this belief; other leaders need to feel as strongly as you do. This will require much of your time. You will need to be less hands-on about the things your team can manage. I know you are angry but look at these incidents as opportunities to teach not punish."

- *How should Helen respond to Hank's feedback?*
- *How should Helen follow up with the Center director?*

Research conducted by Harris Research for Franklin Covey found that 54% of employees say they know the organization's goals, but only 19% can list them. And less than 19% can actually explain the rationale for the goal and share how the organization will achieve the goal (McChesney et al., 2012). What would the results be if your staff and board members were surveyed?

Too often leaders execute strategy through edicts and demands that are ignored or misunderstood and ultimately result in conflict and pushback. Transformation fails when leaders view staff and board members as spectators rather than active partners ready and able to fulfill the organization's mission. The leader's role is to enable staff and board members to execute the strategy. This begins with everyone understanding the strategy and goals and their role in the organization. The result is people empowered to carry out the organization's mission-driven strategy.

Execution requires every stakeholder—staff and board members, donor-investors, community leaders, and so on—to fully understand, embrace, and apply the organization's strategy to every decision big and small. Transformational leaders create clarity for all stakeholder by embracing four keys to strategy execution:

- Relentlessly communicate the strategy at every opportunity
- Focus on what is most important
- Establish an annual plan with clear priorities, targets, and progress measures
- Execute the plan

Relentlessly Communicate Strategy at Every Opportunity

Success requires board and staff members to fully understand and be aligned on the organization's strategy for achieving life-changing outcomes. The best leaders understand that there is no such thing as too much communication. Successful organizations have leaders who constantly reiterate the organization's strategy and priorities. Here are some examples of how board members expressed the importance of relentlessly repeating the strategy:

- Leaders align the organization around a core strategy by relentlessly communicating the strategy at every opportunity as part of every conversation.
- Achieving alignment on vision and mission is key. Leaders must communicate a very strong belief in mission, have a clear vision for the organization, and get everyone on the same page.
- Leaders must communicate strategy over and over, so all board and staff are able to talk about what the organization is doing and what their role is.
- The biggest thing is getting staff all on the same page.
- Strategy provides the framework for driving change, but it needs to be understood and applied across the organization to every decision.
- Our CPO relentlessly communicates strategy and holds everyone accountable for executing their part.

There is no such thing as overcommunicating. When you believe you have talked enough about strategy, chances are you are just starting to get through. Some research indicates that people need to hear something as many as 14 times before they internalize it. Even if it is just seven times, how will you get the same message to every stakeholder that many times and ensure they understand the overall strategy and the important role they play. Publishing the shiny full-color brochure and holding the big meeting to roll out the strategy is an important beginning, but not nearly enough. Strategy execution only occurs when it is universally understood and embraced. Then it becomes the basis for making decisions every day throughout the organization.

Transformational leaders use every opportunity, big and small, in person and in writing, to communicate strategy. Every meeting, every conversation, every presentation, every document is focused on executing strategy. Every decision is explained in terms of how it supports the strategy and mission. This occurs in large groups, small groups, and one-on-one conversations.

Many years ago, I had the good fortune to work with Dr. Ron Fry, from the Weatherhead School of Management at Case Western University to create a leadership program for Boys & Girls Club leaders. As we were working on the program, he said something profound that stuck with me:

"Leadership is about conversations. But they must be the right conversation." The right conversations are about understanding the strategy, how it is executed, how we will work together, how we overcome challenges, and how we learn and continue to achieve greater results. Transformational leaders use every opportunity to have conversations about strategy.

Noel Tichy and Nancy Cardwell, in their bestselling book *Cycle of Leadership*, suggest that the best leaders are teachers. They take every opportunity to share a "teachable point of view" about how the organization will succeed. A teachable point of view describes the leader's ideas for how the organization will succeed and the values about how people in the organization will work together to achieve the organization's goals. But leaders don't just share ideas, they engage in a what Tichy and Cardwell call a "virtuous teaching cycle," which means the learner is engaged in a dialogue. The leader shares the organization's strategy for how the organization will achieve its mission and asks for feedback, creating an opportunity for the leader to understand how the message is resonating with others and to learn and adjust based on feedback from those that will carry out the strategy. These dialogues must be ongoing throughout the organization at every level.

Transformational leaders use questions to engage stakeholders in these strategy dialogs:

- What does this mean for you?
- What challenges do you see?
- What do you need to be successful?
- What do you know that I don't?

This dialogue provides the learner with an opportunity to internalize the strategy. It also provides the leader with feedback and information they didn't have to strengthen the strategy and how it is communicated. These conversations enable staff members to understand and embrace their role in carrying out the organization's strategy. They enable leaders to collect information about how well the strategy is understood and embraced.

This seems straightforward but many leaders fail. Why is it so difficult to relentlessly communicate strategy? The challenge for leaders is to stay on message even when they grow tired of talking about it. In his book *Four Obsessions of an Extraordinary Executive*, Patrick Lencioni (2000, pp. 168–169) states that "executives complain about repetition because they are bored with a message after communicating it once or twice. One of the keys to successful communication is getting used to saying the same things again and again, to different audiences, and in different ways. Whether you are bored with these messages is not the issue, whether employees understand and embrace them is."

Transformational leaders are not necessarily smarter or more talented than others, but they are more disciplined about relentlessly staying on message about mission and strategy. They have the discipline to relentlessly communicate the organization's strategy and help each person understand their role in carrying it out. They take every opportunity to talk about how the organization will achieve its mission. Organizations can carry out strategy only when it is understood and embraced by everyone in the organization. Plans and strategy fail not because they are wrong, but because leaders fail to take every opportunity to talk about them.

Focus on What Is Most Important

Transformational leaders are disciplined about focusing on a few priorities that will make the biggest difference. In most organizations there are many good ideas, and it is hard to say no to a good idea. Transformational leaders understand that there is only so much that can be addressed at one time. They clearly identify and stay focused on executing the few things that are most important and will make the biggest difference. This is only possible if there is a clear mission-driven strategy that makes priorities clear, understandable, and measurable.

Let's check in to see how Helen is doing as she works to establish an operational plan for the coming year.

Strategic Planning Committee Meeting to Review Operating Plan for Coming Year

Helen is preparing to provide the board with the budget and operating plan for the upcoming year. There are so many things she hopes to accomplish in the coming year. She and her leadership team narrowed the goals down to the 11 they felt were most important. Today she will present her operating plan and budget to the board's strategic planning committee for review in advance of presenting to the full board in one week.

Strategic planning committee chair Francis Stillman calls the meeting to order. He summarized the work on organizational strategy and turned the meeting over to Helen to review the proposed operating plan and budget for the coming year. Helen referred committee members to the draft operational plan for the coming year she sent in advance of the meeting. Helen begins going through a detailed PowerPoint presentation of each of the 11 goals included in the plan. For each goal there is a summary and rationale for setting the goal, an overview of the plan for achieving the goal, and a list of initiatives they will take to achieve the goals.

About 15 minutes into her presentation Otis, a new board member, raised his hand. "I can see that much work has gone into this, Helen. Let me stop you and ask you one question. If you could only accomplish one thing next year that would make the biggest difference what would that be?"

Otis's question set off a vigorous discussion about the next steps for the organization. Otis shared, "In my experience when organizations have two or three goals, they are able to accomplish more. When there is a long list of goals nobody can remember what they are, and rarely are any met. When there are a few things that everyone understands more is accomplished."

Helen was flustered, but instead of defending her plan, she asked the committee what they felt were the most important goals for the coming year. Three themes emerged:

- Ensure the safety of everyone involved in our buildings and programs. Nothing was more important than this.
- Increase daily participation.
- Increase individual giving.

At the end of meeting, Francis Stillman stayed to help Helen process the meeting. Otis joined them and offered his help and support. Otis shared the concept of WIGS, wildly important goals (McChesney et al., 2012).

Helen was devastated that the board did not embrace her plan. Her staff members had worked hard to develop the plan; how was she going to tell them their plan was rejected by the board? She only had five days to make changes before the presentation to the full board.

How should Helen proceed? What feedback will she bring to her leadership team?

McChesney et al. (2012) found that when organizations set two to three goals, they generally accomplish all of them. When they set 4 to 10 goals, they generally accomplish one or two of them and the goals they accomplish may not be the most important ones. When they set more than 10 goals, they generally accomplish none of them. Transformational leaders stay laser-focused on the few things that will make the biggest difference to their ability to deliver on their mission. They only set a few goals. They make sure everyone understands and buys into them. They say no to opportunities that don't fit in their strategy even when the opportunity may involve additional resources.

It is difficult to set and stay focused on a few goals that will make the biggest difference. Here are a few examples of how CPOs framed the challenge of being focused:

- I get pulled in many directions. There are always many worthy projects and ideas. I have to decide what to say yes to and what to pass on. Our mission and strategic plan guide my decision.
- Our biggest challenge is saying no. As we have grown and become stronger and more visible, more opportunities present themselves. I worry that we tend to take on too much.
- Every decision is based on what is best for kids. Some decisions may have been different if we didn't do this.

Sometimes organizations let others define what is important for their organization. One of the biggest challenges for many nonprofits is chasing resources that don't quite fit into their hedgehog concept. This can lead to conflict with development staff, finance staff, and program staff members. Admittedly you can make a case for just about anything, but you must ask yourself: is this grant going to be a distraction to the work we want staff members to be focused on? How can we do a better job of presenting our mission and strategy to make our core work more attractive to donors?

When I was at Boys & Girls Clubs of America, I staffed the board strategic planning committee. The strategic planning committee was composed of highly successful people. Many were leaders of very large multinational corporations. Every year when we presented our annual operating plan to the committee, the feedback was almost always the same. "You are trying to do way too much. What is really important?" They encouraged us to narrow our goals.

This was a hard lesson, because there was always so much we wanted to accomplish. And by the time we were presenting our operational plan to the board, staff members were very invested in the plan. It was difficult to go back and make significant changes. I wish I could say I listened and changed right away, but it took a few years of gradual change to become more focused on the few things that were most important. We were fortunate to be able to benchmark the process used by the organizations our board members led. We needed to change the process, so we began the annual planning process with an understanding that in the end we were going to focus on a small number of goals that would make the biggest difference given our mission, vision, strategic plan, and assessment of progress. Our annual plan shrunk from several pages to a single page.

Establish an Annual Plan with Clear Priorities, Targets, and Progress Measures

Transformational leaders establish an overall, ongoing, year-round planning and engagement process centered on what is most important for the organization. The outcome is the creation of an annual operating plan with clear priorities, targets, and progress measures. This is only possible if all stakeholders understand and embrace the organization's strategy and priorities.

Here are some examples of how CPOs described the need for an operating plan with clear measures:

- I always have a plan that is reviewed with everyone. Everyone's performance plans is aligned to the plan. I learned the importance of having a goal that is shared by everyone and how to drive it throughout the organization. I am very intentional about this. I talk to everyone about this constantly.
- We work to align measurements with our organizational goals. I make sure measurements are part of everyone's performance plans. We look at these regularly in one-on-one meetings and staff meetings. If we misjudged the target, we believe it is okay to adjust; some may disagree, but I believe you need flexibility to fix if we got it wrong.
- I believe what gets measured gets done. This was a hard lesson; it is super easy to get distracted. This took discipline on my part to stay focused and make sure everyone is aligned. I make sure measurements and focus on organizational priorities are part of everyone's performance plans. We look at these regularly in one-on-one meetings [and] align strategic plan goals with organization and individual goals.

The goal is a one-page overarching plan for the organization that clearly states the goals, how they will be achieved, and how progress will be measured. There is a three-step continuous process for establishing and implementing a plan:

Step 1: Assess progress on goals.
Step 2: Establish a plan.
Step 3: Execute the plan.

Assess.: Planning begins with an assessment of what is working and what needs attention. Assessment is based on how well the organization is implementing each of the three components of their mission-driven strategy.

- **Mission strategy.** Are we reaching the right population and how well are we achieving desired outcomes?

- **Organizational capability.** Assessment includes systems and process and how well the organization is executing on goals. Are we operating at peak efficiency, and do we have the skills and know-how to implement our mission strategy?
- **Resource acquisition.** Are we acquiring resources needed to implement our mission strategy and achieve our goals?

The assessment should include analysis of organizational data and trends. Information doesn't necessarily give you an answer, but it enables leaders to ask the right questions. Assessment might also include a SWOT (strengths, weaknesses, opportunities, and threats) analysis; surveys of staff and board members, participants, and other stakeholders; a formal assessment by an outside group; or an assessment of organizational capability based on an instrument (see the Resource Center for examples).

Establish a plan. An operational plan that summarizes how the organization will achieve its wildly important goals must be developed with input and direction from staff and board members and other stakeholders. The leader's role is to keep asking questions and ensure the plan stays focused on the few things that matter the most.

To be effective the plan must be understood and embraced across the entire organization. Plans can become so comprehensive and long that nobody knows where to start and what to do. At Boys & Girls Clubs of America we began using what we referred to as GOSIM (goals, objectives, strategies, initiatives, and measures). Our GOSIM was based on a planning process entitle OGSM (objectives, goals, strategy, measures) that is used by many organizations. We changed the order as we defined goals more broadly and objectives as more near-term initiatives to achieve the goal. If you Google OGSM you will find many resources about how to use this planning tool. A blank format for your GOSIM is included in the Resource Center. Following is a definition of each component.

Goals. These are your most important goals, and there should be only a few of them. They are broad but specific enough that everyone understands them.

Objectives. They represent measurable outcomes that will move the organization toward achieving its goal in the next 12 to 18 months. They are SMART (specific, measurable, aspirational, reachable, time bound). There is an art to setting goals and objectives that are aspirational and reachable. Objectives must be high enough to excite staff and board members and other stakeholders. At the same time staff members must believe they can achieve the goals. Having a clear strategy and plan is critical. The leader's role in setting goals and objectives is to keep asking questions and providing guidance to find the right balance. Getting to a few objectives that will make the biggest difference will take some time. It will unlikely occur in one meeting. In the end the staff and board members may not be able to reach agreement on only three. The leader needs to consider everyone's input, but have the discipline to get to three or fewer.

Strategies/Initiatives. These prescribe how the organization will achieve the objectives and should be rooted in the organizational strategy. In the Community Centers of Mission City annual operating plan I have added a column to identify the name or role of the person who will lead implementation of each strategy. It will be up to them to develop and execute a more detailed project plan and report regularly on progress, successes, and challenges.

Measures. These are different from the measures in a SMART objective. Those are generally lag measures. They measure at the end of the year if you were successful. The challenge with lag measures is once you know how you are doing it is often too late to make any adjustments. A lead measure gives you timely information to predict the likelihood of success. Coming up with the right lead measures is difficult especially for participant outcomes. Lead indicators are collected throughout the year. Leaders can act on the lead measures to make needed adjustments.

For example, Community Centers of Mission City has an objective to increase individual giving by 35% with at least seven major gifts of $10,000 or more. Generally major gifts take time to cultivate and most occur in the final quarter of the year with a large number coming in the last month. How will Helen know if they are on track? What are lead indicators? Lead indicators could include measures such as the number of prospects identified, number of meetings, number of follow-up proposals, the number that visit the organization, and the number of prospects considering a gift are predictors of how likely the organization is to achieve its goal.

Following is an example of the GOSIM Helen established for the Community Centers of Mission City.

Community Centers of Mission City Annual Operating Plan

Mission: Work collaboratively to provide children and families in underserved communities with access to programs and resources to empower them to thrive.

Vision: Every neighborhood in Mission City is a great place to live, work, play, and raise a family.

Goal: Triple the number of individuals and families we reach in five years by working in partnership with other nonprofits and government agencies to make critical life enhancing and life-saving services easily available in the community.

Objectives	Strategies/Initiatives	Lead	Measures
By 12/31, increase daily participation by 40% in each Center	• Increase program opportunities for teens and young adults.	• Program directors	• 10% increase in teen and young adult participation
	• Add three new partners to increase child and family access to health care.	• Center directors	• 4% attendance increase/month
	• Increase outreach to seniors.	• Program directors	• 5% monthly increase in senior citizen participation
	• Update and strengthen attendance process.	• Operations director	
	• Explore potential opportunities to expand to West Side neighborhood.	• CPO	• Present board with preliminary report on potential opportunities for expansion to West Side neighborhood by September

Objectives	Strategies/Initiatives	Lead	Measures
By 12/31 90% of parents rate our Centers as safe or very safe	• Monthly safety assessment and remediation plan led by board/staff/parent safety committee. • Identify resources to make recommended repairs at facilities.	• Operations director • CPO	• Monthly assessment and remediation plan for each site • Monthly three-question survey of sample of parents about their perception of child safety • Annual safety and satisfaction survey of all parents
By 12/31 Increase individual giving by 35% with at least seven gifts of $5,000 or more	• Conduct first annual campaign. • Establish updated stewardship plan.	CPO CPO	• No. of new donor/investors • No. of new donor prospects identified and contacted per month • New stewardship program by second quarter • No. of stewardship calls

Lead indicators are difficult to identify particularly when it comes to outcomes, especially when you begin to talk about long-term outcomes. For example, at Boys & Girls Clubs of America we defined the academic success outcome as *graduating high school with a plan for the future.* How do we know in the present the likelihood of that outcome? How can anyone know if an eight-year-old is likely to graduate 10 years in the future? BGCA established on track to graduate indicators. A young person was on track if they missed fewer than 10 days of school, were receiving passing grades, were promoted on time, completed homework regularly, and expected to graduate.

Execute the Plan

"To me, ideas are worth nothing unless executed. Execution is worth millions."

Steve Jobs

Why is executing on plans so difficult? It is difficult because there are always countless other tasks and challenges that must be addressed every day to keep the enterprise open and operating. From the minute leaders arrive at their office (and probably before if they checked emails and messages over their morning coffee) leaders are barraged by phone calls, emails, text messages, voice mail, and people peeking through the office door to ask a quick question, ask for advice, or just to say hello. This all takes place during the meetings and routine tasks on your schedule for the day. It is easy to lose focus on goals and objectives. At the end of the day leaders think, "tomorrow I will get started on achieving our goals." But tomorrow the same things will happen. The same is true for the very busy people working in and for the organization. Somehow leaders must create space for the people in the organization to pursue the goals and objectives that will enable the organization to grow and prosper.

Focusing on the few goals that will make the biggest difference and having a written plan is critical, but not enough by itself. Executing on the plan requires leaders to have unwavering relentless focus. The key is to make goals and objectives central to day-to-day operations and the basis for informing every decision. There are three strategies transformational leaders use to be successful:

- Clarify roles and responsibilities.
- Keep goals and objectives in front of staff and board members and other stakeholders.
- Stay optimistic, enthusiastic, and confident.

Clarify roles and responsibilities. Successfully executing on the plan requires everyone in the organization to understand their role. Staff and board members must understand how they will contribute to the organization's success. Transformational leaders cascade their operating plan through the organization to be sure everyone knows what role they will play and what part of each goal they are responsible for achieving.

For example, Helen has set a goal to grow participation by 40%. The director of operations owns this goal. To achieve the goal all the staff members working at the Community Centers must understand their role. Each Center director will have their own goal for increasing participation. Each Center director must determine what role their staff members may play. This might look something like this:

- The program director will visit every school served by the Community Centers three times a year to promote participation, plan, and host a monthly community outreach event and establish participation goals for each program area.
- Increase participation in the art program by 20%.
- Increase participation in after-school childcare by 10%.
- Increase senior citizen participation by 25%.
- Triple the number of youth in teen programs.
- The center director will develop two new health care partnerships.

The result is not just an organizational plan but objectives for each unit of the organization that are embedded in the performance plan of every person in the organization.

One final thought about how each person's objectives and role are defined. The leader does not necessarily dictate to each person what their role is. Individual goals should be reached through a dialogue that begins by leaders asking staff and board members for their ideas for how they will contribute to the goal. This dialogue enables leaders to discover opportunities they would not have been aware of and builds each person's commitment to the plan.

The role of board members in achieving goals and objectives must also be clear. For example, Helen and the Community Centers of Mission City set a goal to increase individual giving by 35% with at least seven gifts of $5,000 or more. Helen owns this goal, but she cannot succeed unless board members play a critical role. This includes every board making a personal gift, identifying a specific number of potential donor-investors to approach, and supporting soliciting gifts.

Keep goals and objectives in front of staff and board members and other stakeholders. Transformational leaders take every opportunity to keep the plan's goals, objectives, strategies, and initiatives front of mind. The plan and how well it is being executed becomes part of every meeting and central to every conversation through these targets:

- **Staff meetings.** Every meeting is an opportunity to review progress, assess and address challenges, and consolidate learning. Organizational goals and objectives should appear on the agenda and drive what is on the agenda. Data on progress toward objectives and lead measures should be shared and discussed.
- **One-on-one meetings.** The plan for one-on-one meetings should be built on how each person is fulfilling their role in implementing the plan.
- **Publicly displaying the goals and objectives where staff and board members and all visitors will see them.** If feasible, create a visual representation of progress. For example, if the goal is to increase the number of people served, the goal may be displayed in a prominent location along with updates to show progress.

When discussing progress and actions to meet goals and objectives, asking the right questions is important. In general, there are four basic questions to discuss:

- Where are we? Look at the data and determine the questions that need to be discussed.
- What is working? What needs attention?
- What is next for individuals and the team?
- What else is important that we should all know and understand? Is there anything new or different that we should discuss?

Meetings do not have to be long to be effective. A short 15- to 30-minute team meeting to review work to achieve organizational goals can be very effective. The agenda is always the same, each person shares the following information:

- What specific actions did you take in the last week to further our goals and objectives and what was the result?
- What is your commitment for this week to further our goals and objectives?

The answer to the second question is included in a meeting summary. At next week's meeting, each person is asked to share how they fulfilled their commitment from the previous week. This keeps the goals and objectives front of mind for everyone on the team. For this type of meeting to be successful leaders must manage two challenges:

- Make sure all participants share actions related to goals and objectives and not just share what they are going to do this week. For example, sharing that a half-day staff retreat will take place that week doesn't necessarily have anything to do with the organization's goals and objectives. It might be stated as "our quarterly staff retreat will include a full review of progress on goals including identifying success, learning, and challenges."

- Make sure the only agenda item is to discuss commitments to goals and objectives. This is not a venue for providing updates, making announcements, or discussion.

Planning and leading meetings that make a difference is a combination of skill and art. I often hear people complain that they spend too much time in meetings that are unproductive. Leaders take advantage of every minute of meetings and hold everyone in the organization to the same standard. The Resource Center contains Guide to Planning and Leading Effective Meetings guidelines for planning and leading effective meetings.

Stay optimistic, enthusiastic, and confident that the organization will successfully execute its plan and achieve goals and objectives. This does not mean that leaders are blind to challenges and obstacles. These must be addressed, not buried. It does mean that the leader genuinely believes the organization can succeed. Transformational leaders always believe they will get where they need to. Each success helps people believe they are headed in the right direction. Leaders are focused on demonstrating and celebrating progress and identifying learning that can further accelerate progress. They address challenges head on, and they are comfortable adjusting goals and objectives when it is clear they were too ambitious.

Ends Versus Means Goals

It is important to understand the difference between ends and means goals. Ends goals are always directly tied to increase capacity to achieve mission. Ends goals are about increasing impact or increasing the scale of your impact. You want to lead with ends goals. Increasing the impact and reach of the organization is the reason you exist. It will be difficult to inspire people to support a plan that doesn't lead with impact.

Everything else is a means to an end. Means goals focus on what the organization must do to achieve ends goals. Remember part of your organizational strategy focuses on what the organization needs to be good at and how the organization will attract resources. It is okay to have means goals, but they should be directly tied to increasing capacity to reach ends goals and fulfill mission. For example, in Helen's case the organization wanted to reach more people and expand to another community. This will require more resources. One of their goals is to focus on increasing individual giving. Increased individual giving would provide operating funds to target expansion. This means a goal to increase revenue from individuals supports the goal of reaching more families A plan that leads with a goal of increasing funding is going to be difficult to sell if it is not directly tied to an ends goal that supports mission impact. Means goals should always be aligned with ends goals.

Summary

Each of the five truths for transformational leadership presents unique challenges for leaders. Each truth builds on the one before it. In many ways each truth becomes more difficult to implement than the one before. Each requires leaders to continue to grow as a leader. All the work the leaders have done to establish a well-managed and efficient organization with quality people and a clear strategy for success is for naught if the leaders can't move from words describing what they intend to do to actions that bring the words to life and distinguish the organization as one that achieves goals and delivers results. Transformational leaders are obsessed with implementing their strategy and achieving their goals and objectives. They take advantage of every opportunity and use every mechanism at their disposal to reach the organizations goals and objectives. The strategy and the immediate goals and objectives become part of every conversation, every meeting, and every decision.

In Chapter 5 we will examine the challenge for leaders to grow and evolve with their organization. As organizations grow the requirements for its leaders change. Many of the leaders I interviewed believed this was the hardest thing they have ever done.

Notes for Board Members

Board members have an important role in developing strategy, shaping operational plans, and supporting execution. It takes courage to set transformational goals. Staff members need to know the board is 100% committed to their role in implementing the strategy. There are four important roles for board members:

- Keeping the plan in front of everyone also applies to the board. The board as a whole and each committee should determine the role they need to play and make the agenda for every meeting reflect discussion of progress. Boards should review a scorecard and other indicators of progress and offer suggestions and assistance. As mentioned previously one organization organized board committees for each of the goals in their plan. Committee meetings focused on progress. Each committee reported on progress at the board meeting and the full board had an opportunity to ask questions and provide suggestions.
- Board members bring a broad perspective enabling them to ask the right questions to help bring about clarity and focus. The CPO and staff leaders do the bulk of the work to create operating plans; board members can provide valuable feedback and insight to strengthen the plan.
- Board members build staff confidence that the organization can achieve goals with reach and challenge.
- Board members have important roles in execution regarding oversight, resource development, assessment, and providing needed support to ongoing daily operations.

Resource Center for Truth 4

The following resources are available in the Resource Center at the end of the book and will be available online:

- Strategy Execution Worksheet
- Planning and Leading Effective Meetings

5

Truth 5: Continue to Grow as a Leader

"What got you here won't get you there."

Marshall Goldsmith

In his book *What Got You Here Won't Get You There* Marshall Goldsmith (2007) makes the case that the skills, focus, and mindset that make people highly successful managers may not enable them to succeed as a senior leader or as the CEO. I believe this is also true for nonprofit CPOs who have transformed the scale and impact of an organization. The behaviors, mindset, and actions that enabled them to stabilize and begin growing the organization may no longer be what the organization needs to continue evolving. Adams and Bell (2017) make the case in their article "Leading for Mission Results" that "short term success is very different from long-term sustainability and progress on mission."

Some leaders are able to lead an initial transformation. They are able to stabilize the organization, shape efficient operating mechanisms, and build a strong team, but then they become stuck. In fact, initial success may convince leaders they have discovered the one true formula for effective leadership. Instead of continuing to evolve as a leader as the organization grows, they work harder at providing the leadership that initially turned the organization around. This can be a recipe for disaster. Transformational leaders are able to adapt and change their focus as their organization evolves and grows. Evolving in this way is difficult. One CPO shared that making needed changes to her leadership approach after the organization experienced significant growth was one of the hardest things she ever did.

This chapter will provide a road map for how transformational leaders continue to grow and meet the shifting leadership needs of more complex organizations.

Let's Start at the Beginning

Many CPOs described their first months as CPO as chaotic, crazy, very busy, exhausting, hectic, and the most fun they ever had as a leader. How can that be true? Why was it so much fun? When there are many problems, it feels like every time you solve one you make progress. At the end of the day leaders can point to their successes. One leader described their first months as a CPO as very fast-paced and that every day looked different. It was mentally and physically challenging. But every day the leader was solving problems and it felt like progress was being made. It was very rewarding to solve problems and fix broken systems. Several CPOs characterized this time as exciting and fun. One declared, "I loved this time in my career. Now, as a larger organization change and progress take longer. In the beginning things could happen fast." It can be a challenge to move on to a different leadership style once the organization is operating smoothly.

Once leaders successfully build systems and processes to enable the organization to operate efficiently and establish a talented committed team there are fewer problems to solve. The organization now needs something different from its leader:

- Establishing a strategy for strengthening mission impact
- Ensuring the organization has the capacity to execute the strategy
- Building a sustainable revenue stream
- Strengthening and expanding relationships with community leaders

Leaders can get stuck continuing to do what worked in the past. They are unable to provide the leadership the organization needs to grow the capacity of the organization to pursue its mission. Struggling to change their approach to leading the organization, they respond instead by working harder and longer. Here is how CPOs described the difficult changes they had to make to their leadership approach:

- The organization became too big for me to have my arms around everything. I had to learn how to lead differently. I had to empower our team to be great.
- I was more comfortable when I could touch everything. The changes I had to make were painful.
- Biggest change was getting comfortable with not knowing about everything. I felt like I could never leave, never take a vacation. I had to answer every question. I was always frustrated with our team. Everything was dependent on me.
- I believed I had to see everything, I needed to touch every decision. I needed to have my arms around the entire organization. I believed I had led the organization to stability, but as we stabilized and began to grow, I wasn't positioning team members to be their best.
- I put my heart and soul into growing the organization. When someone makes a mistake, I had a hard time. I needed to learn to trust people to do their job.
- In the beginning I had to know about everything.
- I became addicted to solving every problem. It felt like I was adding value. It was extremely hard to give up.
- In the beginning we had few standard processes. I had to be involved in everything. I was very hands-on, giving direction about how to do everything. As we grew, I needed to switch from being reactive to proactive.
- As we developed more process and procedures, I had to change my role. It was really hard.

My Leadership Journey

I will use my own story as an example of how leaders can get stuck and what it takes to grow as a leader. I spent most of my career at Boys & Girls Clubs, first at a Boys & Girls Club organization in Philadelphia and then at the national office of Boys & Girls Clubs of America

(BGCA). I believed deeply in the mission. When I became a supervisor, I worked hard to create efficient systems and build a strong team. I was good at getting things done. I learned how to establish a plan and execute it. I was promoted to a management position and continued to be successful. I changed positions several times. I held nine different positions at BGCA including five lateral moves. In Philadelphia I held five different positions in seven years. I successfully led many of BGCA's most important and high-profile initiatives. I was lucky to have mentors who provided support, guidance, and encouragement. Sometimes they saw attributes I didn't fully recognize myself. Along the way I applied for and was considered three different times for a promotion to a senior leadership position. I did not receive any of the promotions. I was confused about what I needed to do to be promoted. I failed to understand that what got me to where I was in my career was not going to be enough to get me to the next point. Shortly after the third time I applied for a senior position, I assumed leadership of BGCA's training and professional development service and an initiative to develop an executive leadership program, which was a significant investment for BGCA. Strengthening the leadership at the more than 1,000-member organizations was central to BGCA's strategy for building strong local organizations that could grow and make a profound impact.

To succeed we sought a partner with proven expertise and methodology for developing leaders that could be adopted for Boys & Girls Club organizations. After a thorough review of several proposals and considerable discussion, we selected Noel Tichy from the Ross School of Business at University of Michigan as our partner. Noel had authored numerous books and articles on leadership. He had coached leaders at the highest level from the military, government, business, and nonprofits. He led General Electric's Leadership Development Center for two years. Noel was an inspirational and effective trainer and speaker.

BGCA's Executive Leadership Program launched in 2006. It had a significant impact and is still part of BGCA's strategy for building strong organizations. An evaluation found that organizations that participated in BGCA's Executive Leadership Program significantly outperformed similar organizations that did not participate on several key measures of impact and reach (Cermak and McGurk, 2010). Being part of this initiative turned out to be a turning point in my development as a leader. Two things happened that made a significant difference.

First, during the time we worked with Noel we had a regular cadence of calls and visits to review progress and plan next steps. Part of the partnership was that Noel and his team would prepare BGCA staff members to lead the Executive Development Program. This was the only way BGCA could take the initiative to scale. Noel wanted to make sure BGCA staff were able to lead the program effectively. He was relentless in providing feedback and coaching about how to facilitate the program. He was also clear about the role I would need to play as a leader for the program to be successful. Sometimes his feedback was difficult to hear, but I learned a great deal about what I needed to do to become a more effective leader.

Second, Noel helped us to acquire 10 scholarships every year to Linkage's Global Leadership Development Program (GLD). In fact, we discovered that Phil Harkins, Linkage's founder and CEO, had been a member of the Boys & Girls Clubs of Boston. The first year we received the scholarships for GLD, I attended the conference along with nine local Club leaders. Part of the conference was a detailed 360-feedback assessment and the opportunity to meet before, during, and after the program ended with an executive coach. I had a great coach; in fact, he had worked at a Boys & Girls Club when he was in college.

My coach shared a written report of the 360-degree assessment with me in advance and during our first meeting asked what I thought. There was a lot of positive information and I shared that it seemed "pretty good." He agreed there was much that was very positive, but he helped me to see and understand what I was missing. The people I worked with liked working with me, but they were frustrated that I controlled everything. I drove every decision. When people had a problem, they came to me, and I told them how to solve it. I spent much of my time solving problems and answering questions. This didn't leave much time for focusing on the big things that would lead to increased impact. The staff members I supervised were not growing as much as they should because I made all the big decisions. I learned that as a leader I needed to shift from acting as the chief problem-solver to becoming the lead teacher and coach. (If you are familiar with Noel's work you know that leaders being teachers is central to his beliefs about leadership.) I needed to help staff members to become as good or better than me at solving problems and determining how to meet goals. Only then could I focus more attention on what was next and representing our team at the next level. Building the Executive Leadership Program and taking it to scale was going to require significant attention.

Making these changes was not easy. The changes I needed to make were not small. My habits were very engrained. I started with what I knew how to do. I established a goal and a professional development plan. I shared the plan with the people I worked with. I thanked them for their honest feedback. I asked for their help. I told them to "stop me from solving your problems and telling you what to do." I had to learn to listen more and ask the right questions rather than telling staff members exactly what to do. I had to change how we worked so I wasn't at the center of nearly everything. For example, staff meetings changed dramatically. Instead of getting input and creating the agenda and leading the meeting, I had a brief meeting with my three direct reports to establish the agenda. I stopped leading every meeting. We took turns. If it was your turn to lead the meeting you established the agenda and facilitated the meeting. We also created guidelines to make our meetings more productive.

A couple of years later I was promoted first to a senior VP position and then to chief strategy officer. I do not believe this would have happened if I had not evolved from a leader who provided direction, solved problems, and got things done to a leader who helped others to grow. I wish I had figured this out earlier in my career. But thanks to the generous feedback I received, I finally did figure it out. I was lucky; many leaders never do. And all those lateral moves to different services provided me with a unique perspective that helped me to succeed as a senior leader.

Let's see how Helen and the Community Centers of Mission City have evolved and changed and what that has meant to Helen. She has just completed her third year as the CPO.

Community Center of Mission City
Three Years Later

Under Helen's leadership the Community Centers of Mission City's operating budget has grown from $912,000 to $2,500,000. They have grown from 6 full-time to 18 full-time staff members. The organization is now reaching three times as many people. Partnerships with major health care providers have enabled them to open a clinic at each site. An expanded partnership with Boys & Girls Clubs enables them to reach more youth after school. A third community center is under construction and set to open in six months. The organization has committed to building an endowment. Helen has proven herself to be a transformational leader for the organization.

Helen is preparing to meet with incoming board chair Joan Fenz to review the organization's proposed goals and objectives for the upcoming year. Joan became a member of the board just before Helen was hired as CEO and played a key role in the decision to hire Helen. She is about to begin a two-year term as board chair. This is her first one-on-one meeting with Helen as incoming board chair. Joan's goal for this meeting is to set the stage for helping Helen to grow into the leader the organization needs now.

Although everyone on the board recognizes the extraordinary work Helen has done, in the past year there has been some tension between Helen and the board. A few board members have privately expressed doubts about whether she is the right leader for the organization going forward. There are four specific areas of concern:

- *Helen is reluctant to add staff members to support functions such as finance, human resources, marketing, technology, and even resource development. Her focus is on putting as many resources as possible toward supporting the mission. This has caused some challenges. Two large grantors expressed concern about the quality and timeliness of information the organization is gathering. A board member created HR policies and a manual, but there is not a clear plan to implement them.*

- *Helen is always fully engaged in operations. Their director of operations left three months ago. Helen is serving in this role in the interim. She has been reluctant to move forward to fill this position. Helen gets pulled into Club operations making it difficult for her to be present for the rest of the operation.*
- *Board meetings are organized on opportunities for Helen and staff members to present to the board about how the organization is doing. There is little opportunity for discussion and input from the board. Board meeting attendance is beginning to decline.*
- *Helen works an extraordinary number of hours every week. She is at her desk at 6:00 am, seldom leaves before 7:00 pm and generally works several hours over the weekend. Board members believe this is unsustainable.*

Although board chair Joan Fenz and Helen are meeting in Helen's office, they are interrupted five times in the first 30 minutes so Helen can answer questions about a proposal they are preparing. Additionally, Helen took a call from one of her Center directors and every time her cell phone vibrates signifying a new email or text message, Helen glances at her phone to see who it is from.

Joan became very frustrated about the continuous interruptions. She finally told Helen, "My time is just as valuable as yours. I cleared my calendar to commit to a one-hour meeting with you. Thirty minutes have passed, and we have not made any progress. Please silence your phone and tell the staff members working on the proposal not to interrupt you until our meeting is over."

Helen was shocked by Joan's reaction. She apologizes profusely, turns off her phone, and asks her assistant not to interrupt her again.

Joan shared her concerns with Helen. "I am sorry I was so abrupt with you. Helen, you have done an amazing job of transforming this organization. Everything is bigger and better because of your extraordinary belief in our mission, your hands-on leadership, and the energy you bring every day. But you must change some things about how you lead and structure the organization. You cannot personally drive everything anymore. You need to have people around you whom you trust to work on their own. Your time must be spent representing the organization to the greater community and inspiring others to support the organization. We are going to need to significantly increase our operating budget to operate the new center. This is where we need our CPO to focus. You can't do that if you are the human resource director, the director of operations, chief grant writer, part-time accountant, and CPO. You have hired and built an excellent team. You need to trust them to take care of day-to-day operations. If you can't do that the board will eventually be forced to find a leader who can. I know this is difficult to hear. I promise to be honest with you and work with you to grow into the leader we need today and in the future."

Helen was shocked and angry. Her first reaction was to reject this feedback as just one person's opinion. She thought, "Look at all I have accomplished. Who else could have done this? How am I ever going to work effectively with Joan? Our first meeting is a disaster and ended with a threat to fire me. Where do we go from here?"

What do you believe Helen should do next?

As organizations grow, people and process need to evolve to support the realities of a larger more complex organization. This begins with the leader, but it includes staff and board members and even donor-investors. Growing organizations require new infrastructure, new processes, and sometimes new leaders. Each cycle of growth requires the organization to change, add infrastructure, and redefine the roles and responsibilities of leaders.

Here are some examples of how CPOs described their need to change as the organization grew:

* My role changed. In the beginning I had to know about everything going on. Now that is impossible. I need to determine what I really need to focus on. My challenge now is to hire the right people, develop them, build a team and a strong organizational culture focused on our mission, and then trust that everyone can do their job.

- Now I am more focused on helping people solve problems. More of a support person than the doer? I try to surround myself with people smarter than me.
- I recognized that my role in the organization needed to change. In the beginning I had to know about everything going on. Now my challenge is to hire the right people to do the job.
- As the organization grew, I was aware I needed to change. I needed to keep challenging myself by setting new goals for the organization, then learning how to accomplish them.
- The CPO must grow and learn how to run the organization as it grows and changes. I needed to acknowledge areas where I needed to grow. I needed to be open and honest about my shortcomings and ask for help in growing.

Here is an example of how board members described their CPO's growth:

- In the beginning he was not sure of himself as a leader, but as he solved problems, he gained confidence and became more comfortable in his role. He is now able to orchestrate what needs to get done.
- He was able to switch gears as the organization grew, from problem-solving to building a strong organization. He was comfortable with this change.

Leadership Changes

So, what changes do leaders need to make? What exactly must be different? As organizations grow leaders successfully make four major shifts in how they focus their energy and provide leadership to the organization. The Resource Center has a Leadership Changes Assessment tool to help assess where you are on these four continuums.

- **From doing to orchestrating.** In the beginning transformational CPOs may need to be very hands on. They need to solve problems, establish systems and processes that support efficient operations, and assess the commitment and capability of the staff members. As the organization stabilizes and establishes effective operating mechanisms the leader's role is to orchestrate the work versus being directly engaged themselves.

- **From directing to teaching and developing others.** As the organization grows leaders spend less time solving problems and overseeing day-to-day operations. They spend more time teaching and developing staff members to work more independently. As the organization develops a clear mission-driven strategy, leaders work with staff members to provide services and make decisions consistent with the organization's mission strategy.

- **From filling funding gaps to building and executing a long-term sustainable resource development strategy.** Many of the CPOs I interviewed spent much of their first year plugging funding gaps, keeping the doors open, and assuring donors that the organization was advancing while building strong trusting relationships. As the organization grew, CPOs spent more time engaging donor-investors in a long-term partnership based on a mutual belief in the importance of the mission.

- **From focusing on the here and now to developing and sharing a vision and strategy for the future.** As the organization begins to operate effectively, leaders spend more time facilitating the development of a long-term vision for the organization and a strategy to for achieving greater impact and reach.

Four Keys to Continuously Growing as a Leader

It is a challenge to make these changes and to grow into the leader your organization needs. Success requires an intentional approach and the capacity to continuously redefine your role as the leader as the organization grows. Transformational leaders understand the importance of learning and growing as a leader to meet the evolving leadership requirements of increasingly complex organizations.

So, how do transformational leaders manage to grow and change to continuously meet the evolving leadership demands of their organization? What separates leaders able to grow and evolve from those that become stuck? There are four keys to ongoing personal growth. The best leaders exemplify these four keys at every stage of their career. They never stop growing and learning. They understand that what made them successful in the past may not be what the organization needs now and in the future. The four keys to continuously growing as a leader are as follows:

- Make a commitment to personal growth and the willingness to be vulnerable.
- Adopt a growth mindset.
- Continuously seek feedback.
- Recognize and act on what the organization needs now and in the future.

Make a commitment to personal growth and the willingness to be vulnerable. Change requires enthusiasm for personal growth and a sense of adventure. It takes a strong commitment to personal growth and the courage to examine your motives, biases, blind spots, talents and limitations to become an exceptional leader.

Brené Brown (2012) famously stated that "vulnerability is the birthplace of innovation, creativity, and change." Vulnerability is an essential characteristic of transformational leaders who are able to grow to meet new challenges. It is the starting place for personal and professional growth. Vulnerability means always being open to the possibility that you can grow as a leader. Vulnerability means you look in the mirror every morning and ask, "How did I do yesterday? What went well? What could I have done better?" It means asking people around you for feedback: "What am I doing that is working? What do I need do better? What behaviors do I need to stop? What am I not doing that that I need to start doing?" It takes courage to ask these questions. Transformational leaders driven by an insatiable desire to make a difference are not afraid to make themselves vulnerable. They understand they need help from the people who know them and the organization best for them to grow and develop as a leader.

Adopt a growth mindset. Transformational leaders possess a growth mindset, which reflects the belief that people can develop their talents and abilities throughout their life. In her book *Mindset,* Stanford professor Carol Dweck (2006) describes people with a growth mindset as believing their skills and intelligence can be improved with effort and persistence. People with a growth mindset never stop striving to get better personally. They continuously seek new opportunities and new ways of thinking to take the organizations they lead to new levels of impact. These exceptional leaders are always seeking new information and new ideas. They continuously work to become a stronger more effective leader.

This is how Carol Dweck summarized the difference a growth mindset makes:

> Why waste time proving over and over how great you are, when you could be getting better? Why hide deficiencies instead of overcoming them? Why look for friends or partners who will just shore up your self-esteem instead of ones who will also challenge you to grow? And why seek out the tried and true, instead of experiences that will stretch you? The passion for stretching yourself and sticking to it, even (or especially) when it's not going well, is the hallmark of the growth mindset. This is the mindset that allows people to thrive during some of the most challenging times in their lives.

In *Think Again* Adam Grant (2021) describes what he calls "confident humility," which describes leaders who are confident they can achieve challenging goals while simultaneously understanding that they don't have all the answers or even the right information right now. These leaders recognize that to succeed they will have to grow and learn new ways of thinking and doing. They embrace working in partnership with people who have more experience, knowledge, or skill than they do. Leaders with a growth mindset project confident humility.

Nurturing a Growth Mindset

People with a growth mindset take steps every day to support that belief and nurture their personal growth. Here are a few practices that have worked for me as I continue my struggle to grow as a leader:

Reflect. Leaders are bombarded with a daily stream of emails, text messages, and phones calls. Most days there is little time to reflect and take stock in how things are going. It is important to make time to reflect and ask, What went well today? Is there anything I could have done better? What lies ahead that I need to prepare for? How is my team doing? What issues or changes in the environment should I be paying attention to?

Set demanding goals and take on challenging projects and initiatives that expand the capacity of your organization to deliver on mission. People who have a growth mindset establish goals for themselves and the organization that stretch them beyond their comfort zone. These goals should be a big enough challenge to push people out of their comfort zone.

Take every opportunity to learn and explore new ideas. When I have been asked by young professionals about how to succeed, the advice I always I give first is "be curious." People who want to know how things work, who read about and explore new ideas, and who ask questions have a growth mindset. These leaders never stop learning.

Although some people's life experiences may nurture the development of a growth mindset more than others, I believe everyone can learn to embrace a growth mindset. But it takes courage to identify and share what you don't know. A growth mindset requires an insatiable appetite to strive for superior performance and a commitment to seek help. I believe this comes naturally to leaders with a fanatical belief in mission. They understand that achieving the organization's mission supersedes their ego. Here are some comments by CPOs who framed the role of mission in their growth as a leader:

- Whenever I faced a problem I wasn't sure how to handle, I tried to think about solutions that support our mission.
- The mission was always my guide. Focusing on what the mission demanded of me allowed me to grow and change.

When we discussed the first truth—Be Fanatical About Mission—we identified three reasons why a fanatical belief in mission was critical to success as a leader:

- **Passion is contagious.** Leaders who are driven by a fanatic belief in their mission understand a growth mindset is required if they are going to expand the organization's reach and impact. These leaders inspire those around them to do the same. Similar to passion for mission, a growth mindset is contagious. Organizations with a growth mindset are continuously learning how to marshal their resources to increase their capacity and advance their mission.
- **Belief in mission empowers leaders with the fortitude to make tough calls.** Everything begins and ends with mission. A fanatical belief in mission demands leaders to have the courage and discipline to continuously evaluate themself as a leader and make the tough calls about what is required of them.
- **Commitment to mission demands impeccably high standards of excellence.** This commitment means leaders demand nothing less of themselves. Leaders who exemplify a growth mindset inspire people around them to grow with the organization to achieve aspirational goals.

Continuously seek feedback. Leaders need feedback from board and staff members, colleagues, and other significant shareholders to determine areas where professional and personal growth is needed. Everyone has blind spots and behaviors we need to stop or do less of that are holding us back. We also have gaps or deficiencies in our skill set that can hold us back from becoming a more complete leader. One of the only ways to identify blind spots is through feedback from the people who know us best.

Gender Differences?

"In a meta-analysis of ninety-five studies involving over a hundred thousand people, women typically underestimated their leadership skill, while men overestimated their skill" (Grant, 2021, p. 37). Who is more likely to have a growth mindset? Who is most likely to value and use feedback?

When people rate their own leadership skills and are also evaluated by their colleagues, supervisors, or subordinates, there is often a significant difference between how they view their leadership skills and how others perceive their leadership skills. "The most effective leaders score high in both confidence and humility. Although they have faith in their strengths, but they're also keenly aware of their weaknesses. They know they need to recognize and transcend their limits if they want to push the limits of greatness" (Grant, 2021, p. 48).

It can be difficult for leaders to receive the feedback needed to recognize blind spots and identify what they need to work on. It can be easy for leaders to only hear compliments and positive feedback. Who wants to go tell the boss what they are doing wrong? The most successful organizations build a culture that supports feedback and honest dialogue. This begins with a process to provide 360-degree feedback, which is a process that provides leaders with feedback from the people they work closely with, such as supervisors, peers, staff members, and other stakeholders.

There are many formal 360-degree assessment tools available. Some look at competencies and skills; others are more behavior based. This type of feedback can also be facilitated using a more qualitative process. The Resource Center includes a suggested process to gather, share, and use feedback under the heading 360-Feedback Process. Regardless of the format, the feedback will be more honest and helpful when leaders follow a few simple steps to initiate and manage the process:

1. **Demonstrate a genuine desire for feedback.** How people are invited to provide feedback makes a difference. Leaders must communicate a genuine desire to learn from the people who know them best about how they can grow as a leader.

2. **Strive to understand and consider all feedback.** Even if your initial reaction is to disagree with something, leaders have an obligation to the people who provided feedback to carefully consider what was said. Here are some questions to ask yourself as you consider the feedback:
   - What did I learn?
   - What do I do well?
   - What are my biggest opportunities growth?
   - What surprised me?
   - What am I going to do to grow as a leader?

3. **Say thank you.** Feedback is a gift. It truly is. Giving a great gift takes considerable thought. This is true of the gift of feedback as well. Receiving a great gift deserves heartfelt thanks and a commitment to honor the insights provided. Part of saying thank-you is sharing what we learned, what we are going to do to become a stronger leader, and how the people around us can help.

   Seeking feedback from colleagues and friends is an essential component of your quest to grow as a leader. Without feedback from the people who know us best and observe us every day, it is easy to overestimate our strengths and underestimate the areas we need to grow. Leaders who are not finding ways to continue to grow and develop as a leader risk holding the organizations they lead back. Transformational leaders are always searching for ways they can grow and enable their organization to drive its mission.

Recognize and act on what the organization needs now and in the near future. Transformational leaders continuously scan the organization and the external environment to identify challenges, issues, and trends that could affect their organization. They make this part of every conversation. They continuously ask staff and board members, community leaders, and donors for their thoughts and input. Here is how two CPOs framed this:

- I thought about this all the time. I'd go to sleep at night thinking about the Club and then wake up thinking about it. I made mistakes but I kept moving forward. I looked at it like a giant puzzle that I needed to figure out. I talked to everybody, shared thinking, and asked for input. I challenged board and staff to share their thoughts and ideas with me.
- There were no big aha moments—I would sense change was needed and then have conversations to validate what I was thinking. Or, I would have an idea and start testing it with others.

Continue to Learn

I am always interested to observe the behavior of CPOs when they attended BGCA's regional and national conferences. Many of the experienced ones attended very few sessions. Instead, they huddled in the hallways and lounges talking about their operations. They stated they believed they could learn more from their colleagues. Although there is truth in this, the very best leaders, the ones who keep their organization growing over many years, attended sessions, sat up front, asked questions, and stayed after to continue the discussion. These leaders also spent time with their colleagues, but they took full advantage of the opportunity to learn something new.

There are three critical questions for leaders to continuously assess and adjust as the organization grows:

- **When is the right time to add infrastructure?** When an organization is small the CEO, with assistance from board and program staff members, must fill many roles. The organization is not large enough to justify hiring staff members to manage and lead finance, human resources, resource development, marketing, and technology. The CPO must manage these functions in addition to leading day-to-day operations, board development, planning, community relations, and strategy development. Board members with specific expertise in these areas often provide direct support to fill in the gaps. As organizations grow these functions demand more attention. Every CPO and board member I interviewed regretted not adding staff members to support these functions soon enough. Because their priority was always to dedicate more resources directly to mission, they resisted investing in infrastructure. A successful CEO shared the following:

  - I knew we needed people focusing on HR, finance, marketing and resource development. I was reluctant to hire specialists to support administrative functions. I thought all the money should go directly toward mission. I was wrong. At first, I gave existing staff additional responsibility and I tried to fill the gaps. Board members played a key role in providing expertise. Eventually, with help from board members, I saw the need for change. I realized that yes, we needed to be strong operationally to provide superior services to a large number of people. But we also needed to be strong on the business side so we could provide needed support to our operations. We needed to be careful not to create needless bureaucracy.

  - **When do I need to restructure the organization and redefine, roles?** Many CPOs knew the organization needed a different structure but were hesitant to change people's roles. Several indicated that board members were a big help in determining what changes to make. There are two primary reasons an organization needs to be restructured:

- As organizations grow, new positions are often created and added on to the existing organizational structure. At some point the organization outgrows its structure and needs to be reorganized.

- As goals and objectives evolve, more resources may need to be dedicated to the priority goals. This may require a new organizational structure in order to have staff members focused on the most important organizational goals.

Some Leaders Have a Specialty

Not every leader is able or wants to evolve their leadership style as the organization grows. I have a friend who is a very successful leader and has made a career out of working with organizations for a short period of time. This leader is excellent at installing efficient processes and policy, making needed people changes, and helping boards chart a course forward. When the organization is stabilized, she is ready to move on to the next project. This leader is very aware that this is her special talent. She is extremely effective at turning the organization around and getting it on the right track.

- **What are the emerging issues and trends in the community and in my field that I will need to address?** Everyone talks about the need for leaders to see the big picture. But what does that really mean? How do leaders become forward looking, focused on the big picture? Warren Bennis and Noel Tichy (2007) in their book *Judgement* address the importance of leaders continuously scanning the environment, framing and naming the issues on the horizon, and then beginning to have conversations about how they may affect the organization. I believe one of the secrets of highly successful leaders is the ability and willingness to have conversations about the most important topics in the here and now and in the future. Here are examples of how board members described their CPO's ability to recognize, frame, and name emerging issues and topics the organization needs to address:

- Our CPO brings issues and opportunities to the board before they become a big problem. He is able to narrow down from amorphous open-ended to something specific that the board can discuss, address, and act on.
- The CPO is able to help the board to look backward and look forward at the same time.

Let's eavesdrop on Helen's next meeting with board chair Joan Fenz.

Joan and Helen agreed they would meet for breakfast every two weeks. Joan emphasized that she was always available, but she wanted to make sure they met regularly to discuss how the organization was doing, plan upcoming board meetings, and clarify what Helen and the organization needed from her. Their last meeting ended with Joan telling Helen that she needed to figure out how to grow into the leader the organization needed now. Her feedback was precipitated by their meeting being interrupted several times by staff members asking Helen questions.

Joan begins the meeting by apologizing for being so blunt with Helen at their last meeting. "Our organization has never been this strong and the board recognizes that you have made that happen. You have grown into an amazing leader. My goal is not to criticize you but to help you continue to grow as a leader. The Community Centers of Mission City is continuing to grow. I believe our mission is now demanding something different from all of us, you, and the board and staff members."

Helen put her hand up to stop Joan, "There is no need to apologize. I was upset after our last conversation, and I was angry. But after I thought about it I realized I should be grateful for your honesty. After our meeting I asked some other board members, some key staff members, and one of our funders who knows me well for their feedback. They all said I needed to trust the team. My role is no longer to be the center of every decision. I need to teach and develop our team and focus more of my time building relationships with other community-based organizations, potential donor-investors, and community and business leaders. I know these changes will be hard. I love this organization and what it does. I want everything to be perfect. I realize I interrupt and spend time micro-managing my team. What advice do you have for me?"

Joan was a little surprised, but very pleased. She was not sure how this meeting was going to turn out. "I am very glad to hear this, Helen. I also talked to a couple of board members, and they recommended I go a little slower. We are excited about the difference the Community Centers of Mission City are making and we don't want to lose you. What do you think about working with an executive coach to establish a development plan for you?"

Helen agreed that would be a good idea and Joan gave her the name of an executive coach who helped her.

Joan continued, "In preparation for being board chair I have been researching information about what makes nonprofit organizations successful. I would recommend a few of these for you. As a matter of fact, I want to give you a copy of this book entitled Five Truths for Transformational Leaders. The first few chapters mirror the steps you have taken to build and grow our organization so far. The last couple of chapters mirror where we are right now. Chapter 5 addresses the need for leaders to continue to grow. The last chapter identifies some of the trends and challenges nonprofit organization are facing. Some of these would be good topics for future board discussions."

Executivitis

A colleague of mine once said that successful CEOs need to be careful not to catch a case of *executivitis,* which happens when the leader starts believing they have all the answers. It begins when they start to believe all the praise they receive. It gets worse when the people around them provide mostly positive feedback. Soon they start viewing their judgments as impeccable. It can be easy to catch *executivitis,* especially if you have had great success in turning the organization around. It is important for leaders to refocus and take on the next challenge. Board members play a key role in keeping the CEO grounded.

Summary

The leadership behaviors, mindset, and actions that enable an organization to stabilize and begin to grow will not sustain continued growth. Once leaders successfully build efficient systems and processes and develop a competent mission-driven team there are fewer problems to solve. To continue growing and increasing impact the organization now needs something different from their leader.

Evolving and growing as a leader is difficult. Not everyone is successful. It takes courage to examine your motives, recognize areas where personal growth is required, and set ambitious challenging goals for the organization to increase mission impact. There are four key attributes and actions leaders must take to grow and develop their capacity to meet the evolving leadership needs of the organization.

- First, successful leaders are committed to their ongoing growth and development as a leader. They have the will and the courage to examine their skills, motives, biases, blind spots, talents, and limitations to become exceptional leaders.

- Second, leaders able to grow and evolve with their organization nurture a growth mindset. People with a growth mindset set high goals that increase the organization's reach and impact. They understand they must grow as a leader to achieve their goals. They take every opportunity to learn and develop as a leader. They read, benchmark successful leaders, seek mentors, and take advantage of professional development opportunities.
- Third, to identify blind spots where growth is needed, leaders seek feedback from staff and board members, colleagues, and other stakeholders. Feedback is used to determine areas where behavior changes and new habits are needed. Making behavior changes is difficult. It requires help from the people you work closely with.
- Fourth, transformational leaders continuously scan the external and internal environments to recognize and act on changes. These changes and the new challenges they present require leaders to develop new skills and knowledge.

So, what do you do with all this information? The best leaders establish a professional development plan with clear goals for their personal and professional growth. The Resource Center contains resources and information to assist in establishing a professional development plan under the heading Establishing a Professional Development Plan, which is always a work in progress. It evolves and changes over time to reflect the leader's needs, the organization's priorities, and emerging issues and new ideas in your field.

Notes for Board Members

Boards members have an important role in encouraging and supporting their CPO's growth and development as a leader. Several of the CPOs I interviewed credited board members with being instrumental in their growth as a leader.

- In the beginning I was very nervous about meetings. One board member recommended I take a public speaking workshop. This made a big difference; I have gotten more confident.

- Board members have built my confidence level.
- I asked two board members to mentor me. One chaired the finance committee; they helped me to understand finances. One helped me learn how to work with the board, plan meetings, and how to talk with key board members in advance.
- Board members helped me to understand that I needed to have a more strategic focus. Our focus now is more about growth, stakeholder engagement, and our brand.

Much of this happens through informal communication. But board members should constantly assess and support the growth and development of their leader. This begins with the hiring process. As discussed in Chapter 1, the interview process provides board members with information about the areas the CPO will need additional support to succeed. Board members should look at specific areas of operation such as finance, marketing, public relations, planning, or human resources where the CPO may need additional support.

The board has the responsibility to establish an annual performance appraisal for the CPO with clear goals accompanied by a professional development plan. I am always surprised to learn about organizations where the CPO is not evaluated at least annually. This is not a good thing for the CPO or the organization. The annual performance review enables the CPO to have a clear picture of how the board sees their performance and provides the board with an opportunity to determine how they can support the CPO's continued development. The performance appraisal should minimally include the following elements:

- The organization's three to five major goals. CPOs are ultimately responsible for achieving the organization's major goals. These goals should accomplish the following:
  - One or two of these should focus on the organization's reach and impact. For example, "our organization will provide counseling for 250 families."
  - One about should project how the organization will become stronger and more effective. For example, "staff turnover will be reduced from 50% annually to 30%." Or, "all staff members will have a performance appraisal completed by February 1."

- One should describe the financial resources that will be raised for the operating budget. For example, "$2.1 million dollars will be raised for the operating budget that includes a 20% increase in individual giving."
- A professional development plan includes the following:
  - A summary of one or two areas where growth is needed.
  - A funded plan for how the CPO will pursue their development goals.

Generally, the board chair takes the lead in preparing the CPO's performance review. The process should begin with the CPO assessing their own performance. Simultaneously the board chair should invite board members to share their assessment of the CPO. This group should minimally include officers and committee chairs.

The Resource Center under the heading Resources to Support Developing a CPO Performance Review provides links to resources that may help your organization develop a CPO performance review.

Boards may need to change too. Boards also need to change and evolve with the organization and the communities they serve. Although the CPO can be supportive and a catalyst for change, board members must take the lead. The CPO's role is to be partner with the board chair, the board governance committee, and the full board, but the board must take the initiative to grow the board.

There are three primary changes that boards can face:

- **Board composition.** Make sure the board represents the community leaders with reach and influence. This can be difficult as the change that is needed may be who is on the board. Change requires board members to take the lead. Here are some examples of how board members described the initiatives they took:
  - The board looked at themselves to determine if everyone is fully committed to the mission.
  - The board understood they were not the right board; we didn't have the right makeup of people. We established term limits, and we honored people's service. We established a profile of what the board needed to look like and aggressively recruited people to serve on the board.

- We developed a board orientation, a job description, and annual board evaluation. We hold members accountable for attendance. We are now more strategic about who comes on the board.
- **Evolve from supporting operations to being more strategic.** Board members may have played an active role in establishing and supporting effective operating mechanisms, but as the organization grows and operates more effectively the board needs to become more strategic. Here is how board members described the transition from operating to strategic:
  - In the beginning the board was involved in everything. Now the board is more empowered at a higher level—they are less hands on and more strategic.
  - Our CPO doesn't allow us to get comfortable; when we are getting to the end of one big initiative, he starts moving us on to the next big goal. He does not want us to become complacent. For example, he is pushing us to explore how we can expand to other communities. This can be a little overwhelming at times for the board, but it keeps us engaged.
  - As we grew and operated more effectively the board became more strategic and focused on governance versus operations.
- **Assume an active role in growing resources.** Our chair championed the board role in resource development by taking on leadership of our annual campaign. Board members who were not willing to participate could not stay on the board.

What About Succession Planning?

There is one more important responsibility the board has, to create a succession plan. Any time a staff person leaves an organization it creates a crisis. When the CPO leaves, especially one who is doing a good job, it is a major crisis. I asked every board member I interviewed if they had a succession plan for their CPO. Everyone answered no. One board member said, "We have succession fear. We are working hard to keep our CPO. We provide an attractive financial package and lots of support."

Succession planning is difficult for any organization and may be particularly difficult for a small organization. In today's world there is competition for the best talent. New opportunities will arise and people move on. Three questions to ask to begin your discussion:

1. Who in this organization is fanatical about mission and has the talent to sometime take on a major role?
2. Who in the community identifies with our mission and has the experience and traits to lead our organization?
3. How can we support their growth?

The Resource Center has a description and link under the heading Succession Planning Resources to support developing a succession plan for your organization.

Resource Center for Truth 5

The following tools and resources are available in the Resource Center at the end of the book and available online:

- Establishing a Professional Development Plan
- Resources to Support Developing a CPO Performance Review
- Succession Planning Resources
- 360-Feedback Process Overview
- Leadership Changes Assessment

6

The Road Ahead: Trends and Challenges That Will Shape the Future

I am beginning this final chapter by revisiting where I began the book.

I believe nonprofit organizations represent the best of America. Every day in communities across America and around the world the hungry are fed, the homeless sheltered, the elderly are cared for, the sick and injured are treated, children are nurtured educated and inspired, the environment is protected, victims of natural disasters receive assistance to rebuild, and myriad other services are provided that make our communities great places to live, work, play, and raise a family.

The collective missions of nonprofit organizations are aligned with beliefs put forth by our nation's founders that all women and men are created equal and have an inalienable right to life, liberty, and the pursuit of happiness. Nonprofit organizations have a strong belief in the promise of America. At their very core the missions and visions of nonprofit organizations are about providing everyone with the opportunity to succeed, prosper, and live a full productive healthy life. The overarching goal is equity of opportunity for every woman, man, and child no matter their circumstances, their race, their beliefs, their age, their sexual orientation, or their gender.

That said, the problems we face are immense and we haven't yet achieved the level of impact needed to make our collective beliefs about equality of opportunity true for everyone. There are two ways to increase impact: (1) attain more resources, and/or (2) deploy the resources available to have the greatest possible impact. Yes, more resources would make a

153

difference, but we also must strive to have the biggest impact possible with the resources we have. This chapter will explore emerging trends and challenges that leaders in the nonprofit sector are facing, what that means for them, and strategies for increasing impact and scale.

Let's first check in to see how Helen and the Community Centers of Mission City are preparing for the future.

Community Centers of Mission City
Six Years Later

After six years as CPO Helen is leaving the Community Centers of Mission City to lead a collective impact initiative for Mission City. This is a bittersweet time for Helen. She is proud of the work she did in building a strong, vibrant organization that is making a big difference in the lives of thousands of families. The Community Centers of Mission City now operate four multi-purpose facilities. Each center is vibrant and bursting with activity from early in the morning to late evening. They now have a budget of $4.1 million and an endowment of $5.1 million. Partnerships with other organizations bring multiple programs and services into their buildings, making it easy for families to access needed services. The organization has been able to demonstrate their impact through a commitment to collecting and using data. This has been a key ingredient in reaching new donor-investors. More important, their data enabled them to discover ways to continuously grow and expand their impact on the Mission City community.

The board has discussed establishing a succession plan but they always put it off. They have asked Helen to provide a short list of the biggest challenges the organization will face in the future. Helen emphasized four challenges:

- *__Workforce challenges.__ Attracting and keeping a diverse talented workforce has never been more challenging. There just are not many qualified candidates looking for jobs.*
- *__Measuring outcomes.__ Although this is a strength, Helen believes they need to continuously assess and advance their collection and*

use of data to demonstrate impact and learn how to achieve more impact.
- **Continuing to nurture and build partnerships and collaborations.** Although this is also a strength, as the community embarks on a collective impact initiative for young people and families, the organization will need to work closely with many organizations.
- **Remaining neutral** at a time when the political climate in Mission City is highly divisive is becoming more difficult.

The board is happy for Helen and the position she is moving to is critical for the Mission City community. But the board is worried about how they are going to replace Helen. The organization is bigger and more complex than when she was hired. Helen grew with the organization. They need a leader who can manage a large, complex organization and will continue to build on their success from day one. The board is wondering how they are going to find a CPO to replace Helen.
How should the board proceed?

This chapter will explore the future for nonprofit organization by examining three important questions:

- What are the trends, challenges, and opportunities that are shaping the future?
- What will be required from leaders to succeed and meet these challenges?
- How can nonprofit organizations, communities, and national leaders develop and prepare the next generation of leaders to achieve new levels of impact?

Trends, Challenges, and Opportunities

I asked the following leaders of national nonprofit organizations and community organizations that support leadership development what they saw as the most significant trends and challenges nonprofit leaders are now facing:

- Jennifer Blatz, president and CEO, StriveTogether
- Owen Charter, president and CEO, Boy & Girls Clubs of Canada
- Jim Clark, president and CEO, Boys & Girls Clubs of America
- Patrick Cisler, executive director, Lakeshore Nonprofits
- Kirk Dominick, president and CEO, World Federation of Youth Clubs
- Charlotte Haberaecker, president and CEO, Lutheran Services in America
- Commissioner Kenneth Hodder, national commander, The Salvation Army
- Undraye Howard, senior vice president, diversity, equity and inclusion, Social Current
- Stephanie Hull, president and CEO, Girls Inc.
- Jody Levison-Johnson, president and CEO, Social Current
- Suzanne McCormick, president and CEO, YMCA of the USA
- Jonathan Reckford, CEO, Habitat for Humanity International
- Jennifer Sirangelo, president and CEO, National 4-H Council
- Artis Stevens, president and CEO, Big Brothers Big Sisters of America
- Schroeder Stribling, president and CEO, Mental Health America
- Wendy Thomas, president and CEO, Leadership Tulsa

They were nearly unanimous in naming four challenges nonprofit leaders must address and navigate in the years ahead. Each of these represent a challenge and an opportunity:

- Workforce challenges: finding and keeping talented staff
- Collaborations, partnerships, and collective impact
- Data and outcome measurement
- Divisive political climate

Workforce challenges. People's expectations of work is changing. Nonprofit leaders must be at the forefront of defining the future of work in order to attract and keep talented people. Having the right people is critical to the success of nonprofit organizations. It is no surprise that nonprofit leaders are concerned about finding, hiring, and retaining talented, dedicated people to drive mission impact. The success of nonprofit organizations is dependent on having mission-driven people with the skill, knowledge, and desire to make a difference. In today's competitive environment it is more essential than ever that leaders develop a comprehensive people strategy.

Here is a sample of how the national leaders I interviewed framed workforce challenges:

- Our workforce challenges are not short term; we need a sound strategy for addressing.
- Leaders are worried they cannot find people. It is particularly difficult to find frontline staff. Leaders need to understand the future of work and what it can look like in their organization.
- It is difficult to find and retain people with the skills and competencies needed to make a difference. Competition for top talent is steep.
- It is difficult to retain talented people. Younger staff don't want to be underpaid and they want more work-life balance.
- We are competing with each other for talent. This impacts pay, benefits, and cultural changes to support and meet the expectations of younger staff.
- COVID has changed the workforce. Staff want emotional and financial support to succeed. People are less likely to take less pay for emotionally trying work.
- How are we going to hire and keep people with the skills and mindset we need? We need to examine salaries, benefits and how we establish a caring, creative culture.
- Our competition is not just other nonprofits. I have never seen a time when so many of our most talented staff are being recruited by for-profit companies.
- Recruiting and retaining a strong team has never been more difficult. We need to create a culture that inspires and connects people.
- Finding and retaining quality staff has never been more difficult. This is a crisis at the present time. Need to start helping young people see this as a viable career.

- To compete for talented people who can deliver on mission nonprofits must increase salary and benefits.

Workforce challenges started before the COVID pandemic. According to a report from the U.S. Chamber of Commerce there was already a shortage of workers with 5.5 million seeking employment for 7.5 million jobs. Presently there are "10 million job openings in the U.S. but only around 6 million unemployed workers" (U.S. Chamber of Commerce, 2022).

The nonprofit sector is experiencing the same challenge. A report prepared by the National Council of Nonprofits (2021) based on a survey of 1,000 nonprofit leaders found that nonprofit organizations were experiencing an unprecedented level of staff vacancies:

- 34% of the organizations had vacancies between 10% and 19%
- 26% had vacancies between 20% and 29%
- 16% had vacancies of more than 30%

Staff shortages are driven by changes in demographics, access to childcare, and lifestyle changes related to the pandemic.

- According to a report from the Heritage Foundation (Greszler, 2022) "The big story is a 9.2% drop in employment among workers ages 65 and older and a 3.0% decline among workers ages 20 to 24."
- A recent article in the *New York Times* (Goldstein, 2022) chronicles the exodus of childcare workers leaving for higher paid positions stocking shelves or cleaning offices.
- Many leaders noted that staff members' expectations about freedom to work from home, having a flexible schedule, and more work-life balance is important for employee satisfaction. Many organizations are working to change cultures and policies to make them a very attractive workplace.

Vacancies and the challenge to fill them have a profound impact on the ability to achieve our missions. Of the organizations surveyed by the National Council of Nonprofits (2021) 26% reported having a waiting list for services and 21% indicated they didn't have a waiting list because they were no longer accepting new clients or referrals. Meeting the demands for services and increased caseloads may lead to increased stress and burnout for overtaxed staff members, which may lead to more turnover.

So, what are leaders going to do? I don't believe there is a short-term solution to fix everything on a national scale beyond each organization working hard to attract and keep the most talented people available. The challenge with this solution is it sets up a battle for talent. Nonprofit organizations compete with each other for talent; every organization's gain is another organization's loss. Some organizations will be winners and others losers. And our competition for talented people is bigger than just other nonprofits; it includes businesses and government. For many organizations the stakes are high. The Forbes Nonprofit Council (2019) suggests the entire nonprofit sector may suffer. "The gap that exists between the number of available jobs and potential employees is understandably concerning, and some experts suggest that the nonprofit sector might suffer soon due to this lack of skilled talent." This is a crisis that threatens the nonprofit sector's ability to make a difference for millions of people. Leaders must engage board members, funders, and stakeholders in a dialogue about how the nonprofit sector attracts and keeps talented people. We will explore possible steps nonprofit organizations can take on their own and how nonprofits can work together.

Increased salaries and benefits. Several national leaders noted the need to pay higher wages in order to attract and keep talented people who can deliver our mission. This creates a dilemma for leaders in the short term. Increasing salaries or benefits requires additional resources or hiring fewer staff members. In theory decreasing staff members will have an impact on how much of the mission the organization can deliver but having four great experienced staff members may make a bigger difference than five staff members who don't stay with the organization long. A few leaders noted that the larger, more successful organizations were better positioned to increase salaries and benefits. Wendy Thomas, CEO, Leadership Tulsa, observed that "larger organizations are beginning to pay higher salaries to attract and keep staff." This trend will make it more difficult for smaller nonprofits to complete for talented people. To successfully increase salary and benefits, leaders will need to engage funders in a dialogue about the importance of addressing workforce challenges. Stephanie Hull, CEO of

Girls Inc., notes that if we are "serious about paying more, we will need to cut staff and pay those still there more or set a target and put new revenue toward salaries."

Investment in professional development. Many of the national leaders interviewed noted that nonprofits often struggle to invest in professional development at the level needed to ensure staff members have the skills and information needed to provide services at a level that make a difference. This begins with a thorough onboarding process, professional development opportunities to build skills for success in their current role, and experiences that prepare them to compete for promotions. Leaders must engage funders in a dialogue with government and private funders about the importance of professional development to the organization's ability to achieve their mission.

A strong commitment to diversity, equity, and inclusion. According to a report from the Building Movement Project (2022), 31% of nonprofit CEOs are people of color while 47% of the workforce are people of color. According to the 2020 census, people of color make up 40% of the population. CEOs of color are more likely to be replaced by a CEO of color. Professional and board leaders must develop intentional strategies to ensure everyone has the opportunity to aspire and develop the capacity to assume leadership roles. This is not just an issue of fairness; it is imperative that talented and dedicated people are provided with the experiences to develop as a leader. Funders can play a role by providing resources to support professional development.

A culture that is inclusive, nurturing, empowering, and motivating. Several national leaders noted that many young people have a different view about work. They want to make a significant contribution and have meaningful work. They also want a reasonable work-life balance. Jennifer Sirangelo, president and CEO, National 4H Council, noted that to "attract and keep young people we need to build a culture that no one wants to leave." Suzanne McCormick from YMCA of the USA indicated that "transparency about how decisions are made, assuring people are getting the right information and equity are central to establishing a positive culture."

Belief in mission and being part of something bigger than yourself must be built into our culture. I believe more than ever people want to be engaged in something important, something that makes a difference. Our culture needs to focus on inspiring and connecting people to our mission. Being part of a mission-driven organization that makes our communities stronger is our biggest asset for creating a culture that attracts and retains talented people.

Establish a pipeline of young people coming into entry-level positions. There are opportunities to expand the pool of young people seeking a career working for nonprofit organizations through initiatives that introduce them to opportunities for a career in the nonprofit sector. There are four different opportunities to introduce and interest young people to a career in the nonprofit sector:

- **Volunteer opportunities for high school students.** Most college-bound high school students volunteer as part of their participation in various service clubs. Reporting on and demonstrating learning from volunteer experiences is a significant part of the college application process. How can nonprofit organizations take advantage of this opportunity to provide students with information about careers in the nonprofit sector?
- **Volunteer opportunities and internships for college students.** Many college students work part-time and summer jobs at nonprofit organizations. In Chapter 3 we shared the example of how Wings for Kids hired most of their full-time positions from the many students they employ part-time while they are in college.
- **Service opportunities.** Providing recent college graduates with opportunities to work for nonprofit organizations is another opportunity to identify future staff leaders. Service Year and Service Year Alliance are two organizations working to promote and engage young people in a year of service. Tulsa Service Year is an example of a program that could be replicated by other communities and national nonprofit organizations. Tulsa Service Year recruits college graduates for a year of service in a nonprofit organization in Tulsa. The participating students can come from anywhere. Students receive a $40,000 salary and $1,500 bonus to help them relocate to Tulsa. Their website (https://www.tulsaserviceyear.com/) proclaims they

are "looking for the next generation of change leaders. Tulsa Service Year wants the best, brightest, and most change-focused new college graduates to join us on the testing ground of social strategies for a year of service work. Our promise is to help you grow as much as possible."

- **Recruiting youth who benefited from participating in a non-profit organization.** Organizations that work with young people have an opportunity to recruit people who have been helped by the organization's mission.

Nothing could be more important to the future of the nonprofit sector and ultimately for our country than having people with a fanatical belief in the mission and the skills and drive to achieve life-changing impact. The future of nonprofit organizations may depend on finding and nurturing talented people. Nothing less than the nation's capacity to deliver on the beliefs of our nation's founders is at stake.

Collaborations, partnerships, and collective impact. Successful nonprofits will work together as partners with government, businesses, philanthropists, and other nonprofits to establish and execute a plan for the entire community. Working together as part of a community-wide plan and initiative is becoming an expectation. The question is no longer how much impact a single organization has on individuals in their program, but how much impact are we having together at the community level. How many people moved out of poverty? Are more children entering school ready to learn? Has the graduation rate increased? How much have we reduced the number of homeless people in the community? How many people have adequate health care? Have poverty rates declined?

Addressing population-level outcomes requires a different approach to how government, businesses, and nonprofits work together. "Collective impact is a network of community members, organizations, and institutions that advance equity by learning together, aligning, and integrating their actions to achieve population and systems-level change" (Kania et al., 2021).

Strive Partnership in Cincinnati was one of the early collective impact initiatives that has served as a model for other initiatives through a national movement known as StriveTogether:

"More than 300 leaders of local organizations agreed to participate, including the heads of influential private and corporate foundations, city government officials, school district representatives, the presidents of eight universities and community colleges, and the executive directors of hundreds of education-related nonprofit and advocacy groups. These leaders realized that fixing one point on the educational continuum—such as better after-school programs—wouldn't make much difference unless all parts of the continuum improved at the same time. No single organization, however innovative or powerful, could accomplish this alone." (Kania and Kramer, 2011)

Here is a sample of how leaders saw the need for partnership, collaborations and collective impact:

- We need systemic change in how everyone works together; everyone must get on the same page around the big outcomes we seek.
- The problems nonprofits are addressing are huge, the scale of need is enormous. It is difficult for any one organization to make a dent in the overall problem. We must work in concert with others.
- We must have collective conversations about how we work together in communities and at the national level.
- Only by working together can we change systems to make them more equitable.
- We must become very good at partnerships and collaboration. The goal is to work together to solve community level problems.
- There is a growing expectation that leaders will embrace partnerships with other organizations. Partnerships multiply our impact. Success requires a community-wide plan that clarifies the roles of nonprofits, government, and business.

I believe partnerships, collaborations, and collective impact provide an unprecedented opportunity to significantly increase our capacity to achieve our missions. The data show it works and we are just beginning to understand how. Jennifer Blatz, president and CEO of StriveTogether, suggested the following keys for leaders:

- Understand that sharing accountability for population level impact is different from collaborating.
- Everyone understands their role, how they contribute to the overall goals, and accepts accountability.
- Are adaptive, flexible, and comfortable with change. They are able to compete for resources and work together.
- Are very skilled at developing relationships and building trust.
- Understand systems and are able to navigate across multiple organizations. Program is critically important but the need to be able to impact and change the systems is also important.

Every organization should have a plan for how they are going to partner and collaborate with other organizations focused on the same population and similar outcomes. By planning and working together we can achieve a higher level of impact and advance our missions. Ideally the strategy is part of a larger community strategy that involves all stakeholders.

Data and outcome measurement. Since the new millennium nonprofit organizations have been increasingly expected to measure impact. Chapter 3 made the case that organizations must have a plan for collecting and using data to measure impact and discover ways to increase impact. Jennifer Blatz, president and CEO of StriveTogether, summarized the views of several leaders: "Data must drive decisions. We need to build every organization's capacity for collecting and using data to demonstrate impact and foster continuous learning."

Artis Stevens, CEO of Big Brothers Big Sisters of America, noted that "leaders must be able to understand data and be able to draw insights that inform actions and communication. Leaders need to be clear about what impact the organization will have, how they will accomplish it and how they will measure results."

The Alliance for Strong Families and Communities (2020) stated in their report that "members of the human services ecosystem must commit to the achievement and measurement of outcomes in all practices, policies, and regulatory and budget mechanisms. This includes a focus on a common set of outcomes rather than services delivered and core measures with accountability, full funding, incentives, disincentives, and flexibility."

An article in *Forbes Magazine* entitled "Trends for Nonprofit Leaders to Watch in 2022" encouraged nonprofit leaders to "invest more in capturing and analyzing the vital data your organization needs to determine if you are reaching your core audiences with the right message." Nonprofit leaders must fully and completely embrace measurement and be committed to using data to continuously improve and advance the organizations mission strategy. It is our responsibility to the people and institutions who invest in our organizations, and to the communities and people we serve, to determine if we are making a difference and achieving our mission.

There are a number of tools and resources in the Resource Center to help develop and strengthen your measurement strategy. These include Developing and Implementing an Outcome Measurement Strategy, Resources to Support Developing a Logic Model, and Guidelines for Collecting Accurate Data.

Divisive political climate. We are at a point in time where people are very divided politically. Nonprofit organizations depend on support from the entire community. Leaders are challenged to remain nonpartisan. Here is sample of how leaders described the current situation:

- Political polarization is a challenge. Economic circumstances are often tied to which side you are on. Leaders must endeavor to stay neutral.
- Conservative versus liberal and urban versus rural differences make it hard to be nonpartisan. It is very difficult to navigate. This is a significant challenge especially if the organization is receiving substantial government funding.
- Some donors want the organization to take sides.
- Society has changed; we are more polarized. Issues are emotionally charged; it is difficult to find middle ground.
- Currently political divisiveness in the country is very high. It is very tricky for nonprofits to be remain nonpartisan.
- Right now partisanship is very difficult for leaders to navigate. People want to know if you are in their tribe or not.
- It is a challenge to be bipartisan at a time when people have very different views about democracy and morality. Leaders must work very hard to identify what we have in common.
- Leaders must have political savvy.
- It is very difficult for leaders to be bipartisan or nonpartisan.

Effective leaders must be very careful to find space that is neutral not just for themselves but for staff and board members who may have strong political beliefs. The good news is that the vast majority of missions are not associated with a particular political view. Staying focused on mission can help leaders navigate a tricky political environment.

What Will Be Required of Leaders?

Based on interviews with the leaders of community nonprofits, national nonprofit networks, and leaders of organizations supporting leadership development, there are four skill sets leaders must develop now and in the future to be successful:

- Embracing the five truths for transformational leaders
- Business acumen
- Exceptional communication and relationship-building skills
- Agility and adaptive leadership

Embracing the five truths for transformational leaders. The five truths for transformational leaders represent the core of what enables nonprofit leaders to succeed regardless of the size and scope of the organization. The most effective leaders will embody these five truths. In fact, when asked what will be required from leaders to succeed in the future, many of the comments aligned with one or more of the five truths.

Here is a sample of some of the comments associated with a fanatical belief in mission, development of a mission-driven strategy, and a plan to execute the strategy:

- To be successful leaders must have a clear vision about how the organization will achieve its mission.
- Leaders must focus on mission and create a compelling vision and viable path to success.
- Leaders must focus on mission first.
- Everything begins and ends with mission. Successful leaders take the mission to heart.
- Most effective leaders have a very clear sense of the mission and can explain it in an inspirational manner.

- Our biggest strategic advantage is our sense of purpose about our mission. We need to be very clear about how we how we achieve our mission.
- Leaders must be fanatic about mission. They also need to know what they will do, what capability the organization needs to be successful, and how they will pay for it.
- Leaders must get everyone—staff, board, donors—on the same page about how they are going pursue their mission.
- Leaders must have a clear strategy for how they will achieve their mission that is supported by a long- and short-range plan.
- Leaders need a long-term strategy for their mission and a plan to get there. This includes how they will acquire revenue.
- Leaders must be exceptionally good at building commitment and understanding of the mission, values, and strategy for how the organization will achieve their mission.
- Kenneth Hodder, National Commander, Salvation Army, noted that successful leaders must find balance between our spiritual mission and service to the community.

Many of these comments link mission to the development of a mission-driven strategy and a plan to execute on the strategy. Other comments are aligned with the importance of sound systems and practices to manage functions such as finance, HR, marketing, and technology, which are discussed as part of Truths 2 and 3. Other comments addressed the importance of being able to execute the plan. Embracing the five truths for transformational leaders represents the core skill set for transformational leaders, and it begins with mission.

Business acumen. What exactly is business acumen and how does a leader acquire business acumen? I am not sure everyone has the same definition. Leaders with business acumen are able to integrate numerous skills with an understanding of sound management practices, a fanatical belief in mission, and the capacity to develop and execute a plan to achieve their mission. When I searched business acumen online most definitions divided it into some combination of hard skills and soft skills. The leaders I interviewed also generally identified two major components of business acumen. One component focused on the managing finance, technology, data and measurement, and human resources. The other component focused on strategy, planning, and execution. I am going to label the two components of business acumen enterprise management and strategic leadership.

Enterprise management. Leaders with business acumen understand all the different parts of the organization, what role each part must play for the organization to operate efficiently and effectively, and how they all fit together to make the organization strong. Leaders with business acumen understand that enterprise management needs constant attention. Systems and practices must evolve and change to reflect the size and focus of the organization and changing expectations of the marketplace. Leaders with business acumen know they must invest time and resources to manage the organization's systems and support functions.

Strategic leadership. Leaders with business acumen have an inspirational and compelling vision and the ability to work with all stakeholders to create and execute a clear strategy for how the organization will achieve its mission. The vision and strategy are supported by a plan with clear goals, actions, and responsibility that enable the organization to execute the strategy successfully.

Here is a sample of how leaders saw the importance of business acumen:

- Leaders must be able to run the business of the organization. Leaders need to manage finance, budgeting, HR, marketing and legal issues.
- Nonprofit organizations are very complex. Leaders can be overwhelmed if they are not well managed. Many large organizations are hiring professional managers. It is a challenge to grow as an organization without systems able to support a larger organization.
- Nonprofit organizations must run like a business.
- Business acumen is important. Understanding finances is critical.
- Leading a nonprofit organization is harder than leading a business. They need a leader that can manage the business and lead the organization to achieve its mission.

- Leaders need to think with a business mindset and need to operate like a business. Businesses have a strategy for sustainability and growth.
- Leaders need to understand systems. Program is critically important but also need to be able to impact and change the systems.
- Leaders must have business savvy this includes a long-term strategy, a plan to get there, and a revenue strategy.
- Leaders can't be so focused on mission that they neglect the business side.

Business acumen is very complex; there are many components and parts. Leaders with business acumen understand all the various components of how an organization operates and the environment they exist in. They also have the ability to integrate everything with the creation of a strategy to achieve their mission. They are then able to align the organization, board and staff members, and funders on a plan to implement the strategy.

A search online for business acumen training identified several opportunities including from the Business Acumen Institute. Although there are opportunities to learn about the many individual components that are part of business acumen, there are few professional development opportunities for nonprofit leaders focused on how to understand and integrate various enterprise management and strategic leadership components of business strategy.

Here are three recommendations for how leaders might develop their business acumen:

- Understand your strengths and weaknesses, your skills, and your impact on people. Self-assessments, feedback from colleagues, and taking time to reflect each day on what went well, what could have been better, and what was learned all help aspiring leaders to understand how they can grow and develop. It takes the discipline to assess and identify areas where development is required. Suzanne McCormick, president and CEO, YMCA of the USA, noted that "the truth about growing as a leader is the need to be vulnerable, willing to look at self. The single most important trait is humility."

- Be curious and interested in learning about every part of the organization. To develop business savvy, leaders must take the time to understand what is going on in every corner of the organization. The best strategy is to ask people about their work and role in the organization, what are their greatest challenges, and how do they support the organization's mission. Leaders with exceptional business acumen are able to connect and align all systems and parts of the organization to provide maximum support to the organization's mission, vision, and goals.
- Establish a professional development plan. Continuing to grow as a leader is the fifth truth for transformational leaders; it includes learning about all the operating systems in the organization, developing leadership skills, and understanding the trends and knowledge that affect your organization and how the organization achieves and measures outcomes. Your development plan should include participating in learning events. It should also include reading books and professional publications, interviews with successful leaders, benchmarking organizations that achieve superior results and seeking mentors with specialized skill sets.

Exceptional communication and relationship-building skills. Leaders spend a significant portion of their time interacting with people. Every interaction is an opportunity to share the organization's mission, strategy, goals, and plans. It is also an opportunity to gather information. The best leaders are able to quickly form a basis for a relationship and build trust. Here are some examples for how leaders framed this leadership requirement:

- Building strong relationships and trust is essential.
- Effective leaders are able to listen, understand, and put what they heard in context.
- Leaders must be able to establish strong interpersonal relationships with a large number of people. Effective leaders intentionally develop social capital or connections with people across sectors, they can call on for advice.

- Relationship building is a key skill. Leaders must be able to cultivate strong relationships with boards, donors, government, staff, and community leaders.
- Leaders need a high level of emotional intelligence to connect with people from many different backgrounds.
- Leaders must build and inspire trust from all stakeholders, donors, government, staff, service population.

National Commander Hodder noted that trust is in decline across all sectors. Building trust should be a priority for all leaders. He shared a seven-point strategy for what nonprofits should emphasize with the public:

1. Building trust in the organization is the key to a long-term commitment to the organization.
2. Recognize that the desire to give is special and should be cherished.
3. Demonstrate your personal agency, the willingness to act on your beliefs.
4. Reflect on memories of someone who made a difference.
5. Project a strong sense of hope.
6. Share your compassion for the mission.
7. Project a sense of joy about providing support for the organization.

In the end leadership comes down to the conversations we have. One-on-one conversations, interacting in small groups, and presentations to larger groups define our success as a leader. Some leaders believe that it is what they say makes the difference. Other leaders believe how well they listen and understand the concerns and ideas of others is what builds trust. Transformational leaders understand the importance of both. New levels of partnerships and strong collaborative relationships will be possible only if leaders can develop relationships characterized by a high level of trust.

Agility and adaptive leadership. In today's fast changing world leaders must be able to react to change quickly. Transformational leaders must work hard to continuously identify, understand, and articulate future trends and required changes. They build understanding and engage stakeholders in an ongoing dialogue to update strategy to meet evolving needs and trends.

Here are some examples of how leaders of national nonprofits articulated the need for leaders to be agile:

- Leaders must be able to make tough choices about the use of resources. To be successful they must have a clear vision and be nimble, flexible, and open to change.
- Effective leaders must be agile and flexible.
- Digital transformation provides opportunities and challenges. Leaders must be prepared to act quickly.
- Leaders must constantly look outward and inward to lead effectively. They need to be flexible but also decisive.
- CEOs must be opportunistic. There will be opportunities for entrepreneurial leaders who can look outward and inward and connect people to the mission.
- Leaders need a bias for action. They need the ability and willingness to be decisive and take action quickly.
- Leaders must excel at adaptive leadership.

Several people noted the importance of being agile and referenced adaptive leadership as an effective approach to leadership. Adaptive leadership is the ability to link change to the mission, values, and goals of the organization. Adaptive leaders understand that change is difficult but necessary. Successful leaders are persistent in order to bring about changes. Leaders use data to assess change initiatives to learn and adapt.

Ramalingam et al. (2020) define adaptive leadership "as the ability to anticipate future needs, articulate those needs to build collective support and understanding, and adapt your response based on continuous learning." In today's world change is constant. What we knew was true a few years ago can quickly become obsolete. Every change triggers other changes. The best leaders understand this. They are continuously learning, exploring, and testing the ideas that drive their organization's mission.

Developing the Next Generation of Leaders

A recent survey of more than 1,100 nonprofit CEOs found that half were considering departing from their jobs or actively taking steps to leave. Where will we find the future leaders for these organizations? What steps should organizations, communities, and national nonprofit networks be taking to develop future leaders? At the beginning of this book, I stated my belief that leadership can be developed. The majority of this work describes five truths for transformational leaders. I believe these represent the core of what leaders need to succeed.

Here are four recommendations for how communities, national networks, and universities can support the development of leaders:

- Leadership development programs for communities, including classes, programs, and mentoring, can provide powerful opportunities for developing leaders. Community leaders and board members of nonprofit organizations should explore how they can work together to make these opportunities more widely available. Universities, nonprofit organizations that support other nonprofits, and national nonprofit organizations all provide leadership development programs. Is there an opportunity for these entities to work collaboratively to create efficiencies and increase leadership development opportunities?
- Succession planning that looks at the future leadership needs of the organization must become part of the board's ongoing work. Succession plans should include potential leaders in the organization and others in the community who could be strong candidates.
- Be inclusive: according to the 2020 census people of color make up 40% of the population in the United States of the population (Frey, 2021). A national survey conducted by the Building Movement Project found that 31% of nonprofit CEOs are people of color, and 47% of the nonprofit workforce are people of

color (Building Movement, 2022). Board and professional leaders must work diligently to ensure efforts to develop and recruit leaders are inclusive.

• Develop strategies to attract young people to careers in nonprofit sectors. The section in this chapter on workforce challenges outlines steps to establish a pipeline of young people in a career working for nonprofits. There are opportunities for national initiatives that focus on young people volunteering or working part-time for a nonprofit. There are opportunities for communities to promote volunteer opportunities for young people and there are service year initiatives targeting recent college graduates. This is also an opportunity for organizations to work together.

Final Thoughts

Despite the challenges and difficulties, I believe the core promise of America is the opportunity for every person to reach their full potential, to thrive and have a rich, fulfilling life. Across the country and around the world nonprofit organizations work to make this promise a reality. They are supported by, staffed by, and led by incredibly talented and dedicated people— people who wake up every morning ready to change the world, to make it more equitable, healthier, sustainable, and inclusive. God bless these incredible people.

Several years ago my friend and colleague Glenn Permuy (1998) wrote an article titled "The Toughest Job in America." The article points out the many challenges of being the CEO of a nonprofit organization. The article ends with the rewards of making a difference, changing the course of a life, and strengthening your community. Leading a nonprofit organization may not be for everyone. It can be messy and challenging and lonely at times, but our nation needs great leaders who can deliver on the promise of America.

Notes for Board Members

- **Thoughts about hiring a CEO.** Earlier in the book I stated that hiring for a fanatical belief in the mission should be a priority. I believe this is the most critical attribute and without it nothing else matters. But it is not enough by itself. Depending on the size and complexity of the organization more is needed. There are several attributes leaders need to be successful. Boards should look at the organization and determine what is most important and make them an integral part of the search and hiring process. After considering the feedback from national nonprofit leaders, I suggest making hiring for business acumen a priority. Boards should assess every candidate's business acumen. The Resource Center contains a worksheet titled Sample Business Acumen Interview Questions boards can use to hire for business acumen.

- **The importance of succession planning.** Boards should develop a succession plan for the day when their CEO tells them they are leaving. Candidates inside the organization should have a development plan that builds skills and assignments that enable the board to assess their performance. When determining who could be a successor, the board should spend time thinking about what challenges and opportunities the organization will face in the future.

- **Establish a professional development plan for the organization.** Boards and in particular the human resource committee can support the establishment of an overall professional development strategy for the organization that includes ongoing support for the continued growth and development of the leader who is funded.

Resource Center for The Road Ahead

The following resources are available in the Resource Center at the end of the book and available online:

- Sample Business Acumen Interview Questions

Resource Center

The Resource Center includes templates, links to resources, and suggested reading to support leaders to embrace the five truths for transformational leaders. These resources are also downloadable at www.wiley.com\go\mishrell\5truths.

Truth 1: Be Fanatic About Mission
- Board Member Guide to Hiring and Onboarding the CPO
- Fanatical About Mission Worksheet
- Preparing a 100-Day Plan
- Sample 100-Day Plan
- CPO Guide to Building Relationships Conversation Starters
- Suggested Questions for Initial Meetings with Individual Board Members

Truth 2: Fix, Stabilize, or Replace Systems, Practices, and People Who Are Not Working
- Resources for Board and Staff Members to Assess and Build Systems, Practices, and Policies
- Resources for Board and Staff Members to Support Human Resource Management
- Worksheet to Identify What Systems, Practices, and Policies Need to Be Fixed, Repaired, or Replaced
- Suggested Interview Questions Related to Mission and Motivation

Truth 3: Establish a Mission-Driven Strategy
- Strategy Development Worksheet
- Strategy Development Process Overview and Questions for Leaders

- Strategy Development Process
- Developing and Implementing an Outcome Measurement Strategy
- Resources to Support Developing a Logic Model
- Recommended Reading About Measurement
- Logic Model Template
- Resources to Guide Selecting Indicators
- Guidelines for Collecting Accurate Data
- Resource Development Resources

Truth 4: Execution Drives Results
- Strategy Execution Worksheet
- Planning and Leading Effective Meetings

Truth 5: Continue to Grow as a Leader
- Establishing a Professional Development Plan
- Resources to Support Developing a CPO Performance Review
- Succession Plan Resources
- 360-Feedback Process Overview
- Leadership Changes Assessment

The Road Ahead
- Sample Business Acumen Interview Questions

Note to the readers: Many of the resources contain links to websites where you can find valuable tools. Because websites are updated frequently the link may not take you directly to the page desired. If that happens go to the home page and search for the resource you are looking for.

Truth 1: Be Fanatic About Mission
Board Member Guide to Hiring and Onboarding the CEO

Hiring a CPO is the most important decision boards have to make. Finding the right leader makes all the difference. The following information will help guide the hiring process and to create an onboarding plan. Developing and following through with a comprehensive onboarding plan is just as important as making the right hire.

Hiring

Following are suggestions for boards when hiring a mission-driven CEO. Most important, start and end your search by maintaining your focus on your organization's mission. Believing deeply in the mission is not enough by itself, but it is a prerequisite for everything else. Leaders must make difficult decisions about people, strategy, and resources. Mission provides the edge needed to make these choices.

- Assess the situation; be honest about the challenges the organization faces. Ask yourself:
  - What does our organization need most in a leader right now?
  - What are our biggest challenges?
  - What will it take to resolve them?
- Be clear about expectations for what the CEO needs do to be successful and what resources they will have to work with.
- Hire for potential as well as experience. Determine what the candidate could bring to the organization that would make a difference? One board chair shared, "We can teach the technical pieces of the job, but qualities such as belief in the mission, drive, work ethic, and integrity cannot be taught. We need to hire for these first."
- Seek help. Possible places to find someone to support the board's hiring process include the following:
  - University faculty members
  - HR departments at local businesses, hospitals, colleges, or school districts

- Firms that support nonprofit organizations, such as BoardSource (a nonprofit organization that provides resources, tools, and support to nonprofit boards)
- Prepare interview questions that reflect your priorities. Ask questions to gauge interviewees' commitment to the organization's mission and their desire to make a difference. Here are a few ideas:
  - Tell us about a time you made an important decision based on the mission of the organization? What was the decision? How did mission affect your thinking? What was the outcome? What did you learn about yourself as a leader and about how to make difficult decisions in the future?
  - What influenced you to apply for this position? What do you hope to accomplish?
  - How would you describe your belief in our mission? What most excites you about it? Where does your commitment to our mission come from?
  - Tell us about a time when you succeeded in meeting a goal that was very challenging. What was the goal? Why was it difficult? What steps did you take? What challenges did you need to overcome?
- Prepare interview questions to assess interviewees' ability to learn and determine where they will need the most support.
  - What parts of the job do you feel will be easiest for you? Why?
  - What parts of the position do you feel will be most challenging? Why? How will you meet these challenges?
  - Tell us about a time when you needed to develop a new skill to be successful. What was the situation? How did you determine you needed to develop a new skill? How did you approach developing the skill? What was the result?

There will not be a perfect candidate; the board must determine what is most important for the organization right now and determine how to support the leader they choose.

Onboarding

The board's work does not end when the new CEO is hired. Too often the CEO is hired and turned loose with little support from the board. This can lead to disaster.

- To successfully onboard a new CEO, the board must have a clear assessment of the organization's challenges and strengths. The board chair and appropriate committee chairs should provide guidance and support for helping the CEO discover how the organization currently functions and develop priorities for what needs to be addressed.
- Be clear about expectations for the CEO in the near term. Develop milestones for the first week, first month, and first quarter. Set up frequent meetings with the board chair to review progress.
- Organize board members to set up introductory meetings with key stakeholders in the community, including donors, government officials, community leaders, and business owners. This is especially important if the CEO is relocating to the community.
- Define the roles board members will play in supporting the CEO by providing functional expertise. If additional expertise is needed, this presents an opportunity to recruit a new board member.
- Suggest that the CEO ask staff and board members and other stakeholders what the mission means to them as part of their initial conversation. (In Chapter 3 we discuss mission and strategy in detail.)

Resources to Support Hiring a CPO

The book published by BoardSource, *Chief Executive Transitions: How to Hire and Support a Nonprofit CEO* is a comprehensive guide for hiring and onboarding a new CEO. The book includes tools to support your process that includes time lines, checklists, job descriptions, templates, worksheets, and sample letters.

https://boardsource.org/product/chief-executive-transitions-second-edition/

This short article from BoardSource entitled "Top Five Ways to Mess up Hiring the Right CEO" might be used to begin a discussion with the board to plan the hiring processes:

5. Turn to friends and family.
4. Overreact to the weaknesses of the predecessor.
3. Fail to define necessary attributes.
2. Cast a small net.
1. Rush the process.

https://boardsource.org/resources/top-five-ways-mess-hiring-right-ceo/

Fanatical About Mission Worksheet

Transformational leaders communicate a strong fanatical belief in the organization's mission. Exploring the origins of your decision to serve your organization's mission will help you communicate a compelling story about mission that inspires and attracts others. It also provides a foundation or starting point for making difficult decisions. This worksheet offers a few questions that can help you connect with your passion for mission. Ask yourself these questions:

- Where does your passion for mission come from?
- What people, experiences, or circumstances made you want to be part of a mission-driven nonprofit?

List some words or phrases that capture the importance of your organization's mission.

- First, think big picture—what difference does your mission make for the community, the state, the nation, the world, and why does it matter?
- Now think small—what difference does the mission make for individuals and why does it matter?

Share a compelling change story of someone or something that captures the power of your mission.

Write three compelling sentences describing why your mission is important and how it relates to your personal aspirations.

Share your answers with others and ask for feedback. Keep working until you can weave your answers into a compelling mission story that fully conveys your passion and inspires others.

Preparing a 100-Day Plan

Developing a 100-day plan as a follow-up to your interview provides the board with a picture of how you will lead the organization and will set you apart from other candidates. Although you may start working on a 100-day plan before your interview, I recommend sending this as a follow-up to an initial interview. This provides an opportunity for the plan to reflect what you learned in the interview. In most interviews the candidates have an opportunity to ask questions. Use this to learn more about the status of the organization. Questions you might ask during your initial interview include the following:

- What are the biggest challenges facing the organization?
- What are the greatest opportunities?
- What needs immediate attention?
- What are the most important decisions the organization will need to make in the coming year?

The key is to listen carefully to the answers and ask follow-up questions to learn more.

Make it clear that you will solicit input from board and key staff members to finalize your plan before you begin working. Your plan does not need to be long, one or two pages is sufficient. Your 100-day plan should include these elements:

- **Objectives.** What are the three to five major objectives you want to accomplish in the first 100 days. Generally, these should include developing relationships, understanding current operations, gaining a clear financial picture, and developing a plan for the next year.
- **Approach.** This is an overview about how you will go about achieving your objectives. For example, with whom do you need to develop relationships: board members, staff members, donors, community leaders, elected officials, and leaders of partner organizations.
- **Time line.** You might break it down into first week, 30 days, 60 days, 90 days, 100 days, with clear milestones for each time period.

Sample 100-Day Plan

Overall Objectives
- Introduce myself to the organization and its stakeholders.
- Communicate my expectations, and those of others, about the performance of the organization.
- Take steps to ensure that the organization is financially stable.
- Design the plan for future growth and profitability.
- Communicate the strategic plan to employees, board members, trustees, and donors.
- Begin implementing the future plan.

Executive Summary

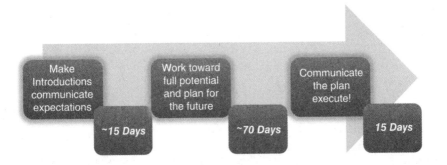

Make introductions; communicate expectations
1. Face-to-face meetings with COO, unit directors, board members, trustees, and large donors
   (a) Begin with one-on-one meeting.
2. All-staff meeting facilitated by outside person (first two weeks of employment)
3. Work toward organization-wide goals (strategic planning process) that can be drilled down to one personal development plan

Work toward full potential and plan for the future
- Analysis of operating structure
- Analysis of organization chart

- Analysis of programs and customers
- Analysis of 2023 budgets for all sites
- Analysis of development plan
- Analysis of information systems capabilities
- Analysis of marketing and communication strategy/structure
- Refocus on organization's mission and objectives to obtain mission goals
- Formulation of a strategic and operating plans

Communicate the plan, execute!

- Brand, brand, and brand
- Objectives and strategic plan
- Resource development plan
- Five-year operating plan
- Board development plan

CPO Guide to Building Relationships Conversation Starters

Every CPO interviewed spent considerable time during their first few months building relationships with board members and other key stakeholders including donors, government officials, business leaders, staff members, and other community leaders. They took notes and followed up to share what they learned. Several made it the focus of their first report to the board. Here is some of the questions they asked:

- How long have you been involved with the organization?
- How did you first become involved?
- What excites you about what the organization is currently doing?
- What do you think we could do better?
- What are the most important things for our organization to address in the next few months? Next year?
- What are our biggest opportunities?
- What do you want your contribution to the organization to be?
- What role in fund raising can you play?
- What do you believe are the major challenges facing the organization? What advice would you offer?

Suggested Questions for Initial Meetings with Individual Board Members

New CPOs should set up individual meetings with every person on the board as soon as possible. Following are some sample questions to help guide the conversation:

- How long have you been involved on the board?
- How did you become a board member?
- What excites you about the organization? What are the biggest opportunities for this organization? How can we take advantage of these opportunities?
- What are our biggest challenges? What should we be thinking about to meet address these challenges?
- What is the most important thing I should be focused on?
- How can you help?
- What role can you play in fund raising?

Truth 2: Fix, Stabilize, or Replace Systems, Practices, and People Who Are Not Working

Resources for Board and Staff Members to Build Systems, Practices, and Policies

One step the board and staff members can take in partnership is an assessment of the organization. There are several resources available to help you do this. Most of these tools provide standards for effective and efficient operations.

- The National Council of Nonprofits web page has links to several nonprofit organization assessment tools available at no charge. https://www.councilofnonprofits.org/tools-resources/organizational-self-assessments
- This self-assessment tool was developed by the Nonprofit Association of Oregon and can be downloaded for free. https://nonprofitoregon.org/sites/default/files/uploads/file/NP%20Org%20Self%20Assessment_0.pdf
- WNC Nonprofit Pathways infrastructure checklist can be downloaded from their website. It is designed to be a starting point for assessment for smaller organizations. https://nonprofitpathways.org/resources/organizational-assessment-tools/
- "An Executive Director's Guide to Financial Leadership" isn't an assessment but is an excellent overview of the role the CEO plays in leading and managing finances. https://nonprofitquarterly.org/executive-directors-guide-financial-leadership-2/
- "The Nonprofit Audit Guide" from the National Council of Nonprofits provides charitable nonprofits with the tools they need to make informed decisions about independent audits. https://www.councilofnonprofits.org/nonprofit-audit-guide

Resources for Board and Staff Members to Support Human Resource Management

Checklist of Human Resource Management Indicators for Nonprofit Organizations: This is an easy to use checklist to assess HR practices.

https://managementhelp.org/organizationalperformance/nonprofits/human-resources.htm

The Center for Nonprofit Excellence provides many resources to support all aspects of managing human resources in nonprofit organizations.

https://7principles.thecne.org/wp-content/uploads/2022/08/CNE-7-Principles-Tools-Resources-1.17.23-1.pdf

Inc.'s "Nonprofit Organizations, and Human Resource Management" provides a high-level overview of major components of human resources in nonprofit organizations.

https://www.inc.com/encyclopedia/nonprofit-organizations-and-human-resources-management.html

Human Resources Management for Public and Nonprofit Organizations by Joan Pynes (2013) has been updated to include the latest information and resources for managing people in nonprofit organizations.

Worksheet to Identify What Systems, Practices, and Policies Need to Be Fixed, Repaired, or Replaced

	Current State	Desired Change
Systems		
Practices		
Policies		
People		

Suggested Interview Questions
Related to Mission and Motivation

In addition to exploring experience, knowledge, and skills, employment interviews should include questions about mission and the candidate's desire to make a difference. Following are some examples of questions that can help hire people aligned with your organization's mission.

Interview Questions About Mission
Send a copy of the mission statement prior to the interview and indicate you will be asking questions about the organization's mission.

- What about our mission is most important to you?
  - Why?
  - If you were talking to someone about our organization, how would you describe our mission?
- How has the mission of an organization you worked for influenced an important decision you had to make?
  - What was the specific situation?
  - How did the mission influence your decision?
  - What did you decide?
  - What was the result?

Interview Questions About Desire to Make a Difference, Motivation
- If you join our organization, what do you hope your contribution will be?
  - How will the organization be more effective because of your contribution?
- Tell me about an important and challenging goal you have achieved.
  - What was the goal and why was it challenging?
  - What steps did you take?
  - What challenges did you have to overcome?
  - What was the result?

Truth 3: Establish a Mission-Driven Strategy

Strategy Development Worksheet

	Outcomes	Who Serve	How
Mission			
Strategy			

Organizational Capacity

- What will we need to be exceptionally good at to achieve our desired outcomes for a significant population?
- **Systems.** How will we ensure we are an efficient and effectively managed organization with the capacity to implement our mission strategy?
- **People.** How will we engage and prepare people to implement our strategy?
- **Measurement.** What must we measure to know if we are succeeding and how can we continue to get better?
- **Resources Acquisition.** How will we ensure a sustainable source of resources aligned to our mission strategy that enables us to provide high-quality services that make a difference and continue to grow?

Strategy Development Process Overview and Questions for Leaders

The most effective organizational strategies consider and conceptualize all three parts of the model—mission strategy, organizational capability strategy, and resource acquisition. Developing organizational strategy is a dynamic process supported by the organization's continuous learning and identifying new opportunities. The following figure provides an overview of the process and questions to consider.

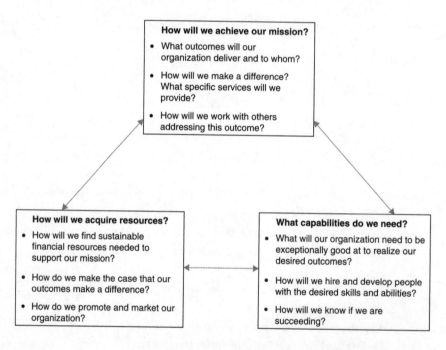

How will we achieve our mission?
- What outcomes will our organization deliver and to whom?
- How will we make a difference? What specific services will we provide?
- How will we work with others addressing this outcome?

How will we acquire resources?
- How will we find sustainable financial resources needed to support our mission?
- How do we make the case that our outcomes make a difference?
- How do we promote and market our organization?

What capabilities do we need?
- What will our organization need to be exceptionally good at to realize our desired outcomes?
- How will we hire and develop people with the desired skills and abilities?
- How will we know if we are succeeding?

Too often organizations spend lots of time and energy working on a strategic plan without having a clear strategy. I am not suggesting that a strategic plan is not important but without a strategy tied to your mission it has little chance of making the difference you desire. A plan should capture the overall strategy and set a few visionary goals for the difference you will make and how many people will be affected. The rest of the plan will work best if it is in two- or three-year increments with the coming year having the most detail.

Strategy Development Process

Every nonprofit organization needs to articulate an overarching strategy and plan for implementation. Success requires thought, collaboration, and action. The planning process and the time commitment will vary based on the size and current capability of the organization. Think of strategy development and ongoing refinement not as extra work but part of the ongoing work of the CEO, the board and staff members, and all stakeholders. It is part of the ongoing conversation that takes place continuously throughout the organization.

Organizations that are struggling or in crisis should have a simple plan focused on increasing operational capacity and legitimacy before investing time to developing a longer-term plan. One of the organizations I interviewed developed a one-page strategic plan that had three components: stabilize, develop, and grow. The plan had a single metric—increase the number of youth that participated two or more times per week. This was easy for all stakeholders to understand. As they demonstrated success, support from stakeholders increased and new opportunities became available.

The overall strategy development process will, depending on circumstances, include three major steps as summarized next. Although the focus is on developing the strategy and planning, preparation and execution is critical to success. Too often organizations create plans that are never executed. We will address execution in Chapter 4.

Step 1: Prepare
- Develop a workplan for developing your strategy with goals, milestones, decision points, and responsibilities.
- Create a stakeholder engagement plan: Who are they? When and how will they be engaged?
- Assess the organization.
- Gather and summarize data about the organization, the difference the organization desires, and the community to be served.

Step 2: Develop a Strategy
- Conduct retreats with staff and board members to develop an overarching strategy.
- Develop a draft of the overarching strategy.

- Solicit feedback and input from key stakeholders about the draft strategy and what the plan will need to address to be successful.
- Summarize feedback and finalize the overarching strategy and operational plan.
- Finalize and present to the board for approval.

Step 3: Communicate the Strategy Relentlessly
- Develop and implement the communication plan.
- Begin to align the organization with the plan.
- Implement measurement strategy.
- Ensure continuous assessment of progress and process to make adjustments based on learning and new opportunities.

Developing and Implementing
an Outcome Measurement Strategy

Here is a five-step process to develop a comprehensive outcome measurement strategy.

1. Create a logic model or theory of change. A logic model depicts the relationship between the services the organization provides and the desired short- and long-term outcomes. Generally there are four parts:
   - Inputs or resources available to realize the outcomes of the program. This includes people, supplies, facility, program curriculum, and program models.
   - Process describes how the resources are organized and used to provide program, services, and activities.
   - Outputs refer to how many people are served and how much service is provided. These are expressed in very concrete terms. For example: 200 expectant mothers complete a 12-week parenting and prenatal care class with 80% attendance.
   - Outcomes depict the impact or difference the organization makes. Generally the outcomes are divided into initial, intermediate, and long-term outcomes.

   The work you did in developing your mission outcomes strategy is the basis for your logic model. You have defined the immediate outcomes related to your mission, whom you will service, and how you will make a difference. (See the next section for a sample logic model and links to several excellent resources to support development of your logic model and recommended additional reading.)

2. For each outcome, determine which indicators are important. Indicators are measurable data used to determine if the organization is implementing the program as expected and achieving desired outcomes. What are those vital few indicators that tell you things are working as intended? For example, if you are leading a program for expectant mothers one outcome might be that expectant mothers

follow proper prenatal nutritional and health guidelines, demonstrated through indicators such as these:
- Knows and understands prenatal nutritional and health
guidelines
- Makes a personal commitment to engage in behavior to support the birth of a healthy baby
- Follows prenatal nutritional and health guidelines; keeps all
appointments with health care providers
- Plans and prepares meals that meet nutritional guidelines
   (See "Resources to Guide Selecting Indicators" for an overview
and links to resources and tools to support development of
indicators.)

3. Determine what information you will collect and how. You may
want to begin with data you can collect easily. Judge the return on
investment (ROI) of gathering data that are more difficult or time
consuming to collect. As much as possible build the measurement
into the program. Build up the depth and sophistication of your
measurement strategy over time. For example:
- For the indicator of knowing and understanding nutritional
and health guidelines a simple quiz can be given to test it.
- For the commitment indicator participants might be asked to
write a goal and establish a plan for how they will integrate
the knowledge they gain into their daily routine. This activity
can be built into the program.
- The indicator of following the guidelines may require a larger
commitment of resources:
  - Participants keep a diary that includes what they eat
  each day.
  - Keep all appointments with health care providers.
  - Refrain from behavior that could adversely affect the baby's
  health (smoking, using alcohol or drugs).
   Clearly define each indicator so everyone is collecting the same
information.

4. Determine what a successful measure looks like. For example, do
participants need to score a 100 on the quiz to be counted as knowing and understanding nutritional and health guidelines or does a
score of 90% or 80% count as success?

5. Determine how you are going to format and share the information. For example, for the indicator of passing a quiz on nutrition during pregnancy you might report the number or percentage of participants that demonstrate understanding of proper prenatal care. The data from the quiz can be used to make adjustments to the program. If a large percentage of participants missed the same questions, staff members can go back and make adjustments to the program. All stakeholders—staff and board members and donors—should play a role in looking at the collected data.

Resources to Support Developing a Logic Model

"Guidelines and Framework for Designing Basic Logic Model" provided by the Management Library is a good high-level overview of logic models. It is a good place to begin thinking about your logic model. One work of caution: the more complex the organization, the more services provided, the more difficult it is to establish a logic model that is clear and easy to understand and addresses the right level of complexity.

https://managementhelp.org/freenonprofittraining/diagramming-your-nonprofit.htm

The CDC website contains an excellent resource to guide the process of developing a logic model and engaging stakeholders. The Program Evaluation Framework Checklist is located here:

https://www.cdc.gov/eval/steps/step2/index.htm

The University of Wisconsin Extension website contains a comprehensive set of tools, information, and templates to develop a logic model. The site includes step-by-step guides, as well as a syllabus for a training program.

https://fyi.extension.wisc.edu/programdevelopment/logic-models/

The Community Tool Box provided by the Center for Community Health and Development at University of Kansas offers a resource entitled "Developing a Logic Model or Theory of Change," which provides an overview of what a logic model is, how to create a logic model and how to use a logic model.

https://ctb.ku.edu/en/table-of-contents/overview/models-for-community-health-and-development/logic-model-development/main

The Compass website How to Develop a Logic Model provides an easy to follow seven-step process for developing a logic model.

https://www.thecompassforsbc.org/how-to-guides/how-develop-logic-model-0

Recommended Reading About Measurement

Measuring Performance in Public and Nonprofit Organizations: An Integrated Approach by Theodore H. Poister, Maria P. Aristigueta, and Jeremy Hall (San Francisco: Jossey-Bass, 2015). This book has a wealth of information about performance management in government and nonprofit organizations including information on developing a logic model, selecting indicators, collecting data, presenting data, and using data for performance management and planning.

Leap of Reason: Managing to Outcomes in an Era of Scarcity by Mario Morino (Washington, DC: Venture Philanthropy Partners, 2011). This book provides inspiration and direction for leaders to establish meaningful measurement strategies. It is based on the experiences of philanthropist Mario Morino, McKinsey & Company, and other experts.

Measure What Matters: How Google, Bono and the Gates Foundation Rock the World with OKRs by John Doerr (New York: Portfolio/Penguin, 2018). This book is not written specifically for nonprofit leaders, but it makes the strong case that measurement matters to the mission of the organization.

Logic Model Template

Inputs/ Resources	Activities	Outputs	Initial Outcomes	Intermediate Outcomes	Long- Term Outcomes

Resources to Guide Selecting Indicators

This resource provided by the CDC Program Performance Office defines input, process, and outcome indicators as well as links to other websites including a site entitled Criteria for Selection of High-Performing Indicator. https://www.cdc.gov/evaluation/logicmodels/index.htm

This resource from the SROI project in the UK entitled "Guidance on Choosing Indicators of Outcomes" provides an excellent overview broken down into these topics:

- The basics
- What kinds of indicators should I use?
- Knowing when an indicator is appropriate
- Best practice and checklist

https://socialvalueuk.org/resource/choosing-outcome-indicators/

The Outcome Indicators Project is a joint effort of the Urban Institute and the Center for What Works. It provides information and resource to support developing a measurement strategy. It provides numerous examples of outcomes and indicators for a variety of programs.
https://www.urban.org/policy-centers/cross-center-initiatives/performance-management-measurement/projects/nonprofit-organizations/projects-focused-nonprofit-organizations/outcome-indicators-project

Analyzing Outcome Information from the Urban Institute provides a step-by-step guide to analyze and use outcome information.
https://www.urban.org/research/publication/analyzing-outcome-information

Guidelines for Collecting Accurate Data

Accurate data are critical to support all components of your organizational strategy and to making good decisions and communicating accurate results. The cost to an organization of having its data questioned is high. Following are four steps to ensure that you have accurate data. The key is to provide exceptional clarity about each step:

1. Determine what information is needed and clearly define the terms.
2. Clearly define the process and procedures for collecting and storing information.
3. Train and thoroughly prepare staff to collect the information.
4. Check and recheck your information at every stage.

Resource Development Resources

National Council of Nonprofit Organizations contains tools and information about resource development.

https://www.councilofnonprofits.org/tools-resources-categories/fundraising

Association for Fundraising Professionals is a membership organization for resource development professionals. The offer a variety of training, tools, and resources.

https://afpglobal.org/

Indiana Center on Philanthropy offers numerous professional development opportunities many of them available online. The site also contains a series of white papers that address a variety of topics related to resource development.

https://www.learningtogive.org/resources/center-philanthropy-indiana-university

The IU Lilly Family School of Philanthropy. The Fund Raising School offers 20 courses, 5 certificates, and customized training designed to bolster your fundraising efforts.

https://philanthropy.iupui.edu/professional-development/fundraising-school/index.html

Nonprofitready.org offers free online courses, videos, and how-to guides to help develop your fund raising skills.

https://www.nonprofitready.org/

Fundraising Academy mission is to help nonprofits to significantly increase their fundraising capabilities and the impact they have in their communities and society through a proven contemporary curriculum presented by world-class nonprofit leaders, best-in-class faculty members, and renowned philanthropists.

fundraising-academy.org

The National Council of Nonprofits produces and curates tools, resources, and samples for nonprofits. View the most recent additions, browse by category or tag, or search for the specific information you are looking for.

https://www.councilofnonprofits.org/tools-resources-tags/Fundraising

Truth 4: Executing Drives Results

Strategy Execution Worksheet

1. **Relentlessly communicate the strategy at every opportunity over and over and over again.**

   Make a list of all the opportunities you have to talk about strategy.

2. **Focus on what is most important.**

   How will you communicate two most important things for your club to be focused on right now to different audiences?

3. **Establish an annual plan with clear priorities, targets, and progress measures.**

   Lag measures: How will you know if you have been successful?
   Lead measures: What will you measure to be sure you are on track along the way?

4. **Execute the plan.**

   How will you make your goals part of every decision, every discussion, and every meeting?

Planning and Leading
Effective Meetings

We spend a great deal of our time in meetings of one kind or another. Often these meetings fail to achieve their purpose. When talking about how to lead effective meetings I often ask leaders, how much of your time do you waste in meetings? The answer is usually about 40% to 50% of time spent in meetings is wasted. Imagine the impact if we can even cut that time in half.

Time spent together is precious, and transformational leaders take every possible advantage of this time. The key to successful meetings is effective planning, being disciplined about how the meeting is conducted, and following through to make sure decisions made at the meeting are implemented.

Planning the meeting and setting the agenda. Effective meetings begin with planning.

- Ask for input from participants about agenda items. If there are too many items, prioritize what is most important.
- Have an overall objective for the meeting and an objective for each agenda item that clarifies the desired outcome. Clarifying the outcome for each agenda item helps focus the discussion. Even updates should be clear about the result. The objective might be "everyone understands progress to date, next steps, and the role each person must play."
- The agenda should establish a specific amount to time for each agenda item.
- Make sure there is sufficient time to discuss the most important items, which are frequently planned for the end of the meeting. The idea is we will end with what is most important. The problem is that several agenda items take longer than planned and the most important agenda item receives little attention.
- If discussion is required plan a process for how the discussion will be conducted and outlined. The process should support broad participation and a clear path to making a decision and clarifying next steps.

- Determine if prereading is required and include with agenda. Make it clear that everyone is expected to have reviewed the material.

Facilitating the meeting. Set ground rules. Start and end on time. One person at a time talks. Stick to time allotted. Establish roles: time keeper, assign someone to keep track of decisions made, and someone to provide feedback.

- Enforce ground rules and time allotments for each agenda item. This doesn't mean you can never spend more time than allotted on an agenda item if the discussion is important and more time is needed. But before proceeding determine what agenda items are going to be shortened or eliminated.
- Keep people on track. There is a tendency for discussions to get off topic or to focus on a small point and then avoid addressing the big questions. Leaders help keep the discussion on track.
- Ask for feedback. This does not have to be complicated. Ask three questions:
  - What percentage of the meeting was valuable?
  - What was the best thing about the meeting?
  - What would have made the meeting more effective?

Follow-up
- Send out a summary of decisions made, who is responsible for carrying them out, and a time line for implementing them.
- Send out a summary of feedback along with any learning about how to make the next meeting more productive.

Truth 5: Continue to Grow as a Leader

Establishing a Professional Development Plan

When we talked about setting organizational goals, we suggested that the secret was the fewer the better. The same is true for your professional development goals. I suggest that one of your goals is always to remain current about the issues, challenges, and new ideas in nonprofit management and leadership and advances in the field your mission addresses. For example, if you are an organization that provides family counseling, how will you keep up with this field? Your plan might involve subscribing to professional journals, reading, benchmarking.

Here are five questions to ask to help establish a professional development plan:

- How will I keep current on issues related to our mission and trends and challenges for nonprofit organizations?
- Based on our strategy and plan are there areas I need to learn more about?
- How will I get feedback to identify blind spots I need to work on? What will I do with the results?
- What does my team need from me in the coming year to be successful?
- What support do I need?

Resources to Support Developing a CPO Performance Review

Leading Governance. We help improve leadership, management, and performance in organizations by supporting the development of boards, board members, and governance processes. https://leadinggovernance.com/

Appraising the CEO. "A Performance Review—Appraising the CEO." https://leadinggovernance.com/blog/ceo-performance-review/

Board Source (https://boardsource.org). Board Source has a wide range of tools and resources to support nonprofit board effectiveness and support increase organizational impact. This includes a resource for assessing the chief executive. https://boardsource.org/product/assessment-chief-executive

Succession Planning Resources

Annie E. Casey Foundation. Building Leaderful Organizations: Succession Planning for Nonprofits provides a framework for board and staff leaders to approach succession planning. https://assets.aecf.org/m/resourcedoc/AECF-BuildingLeaderfulOrganizations-2008-Full.pdf

This toolkit provided by the Federal Reserve Bank of Kansas City helps board and professional leaders to develop a comprehensive succession plan. https://www.kansascityfed.org/community/nonprofit-succession-toolkit/

This resource from the University of Washington provides a step-by-step guide to developing a succession plan with tools and directions to support each step. https://hr.uw.edu/pod/wp-content/uploads/sites/10/2018/08/Succession-Planning-Toolkit.pdf

360-Feedback Process

It is critical for leaders to receive honest, helpful feedback about their performance from staff and board members, investors, and colleagues you work with from other organizations. There are many excellent tools and instruments available to facilitate this, but it can also be as simple as asking a few key questions of the people you work closely with.

Following is a template for asking 360 feedback that can be done easily and inexpensively.

You can use paper and pencil as indicated in the memo or could create a Google Doc and invite people to share their thoughts.

Here is an outline of the message to send asking for feedback.

To:
From:

Subject: 360-degree Feedback

I am striving to continue to grow as a leader and I need your help. I need feedback from the people I work closely with to **develop and grow as a leader. Please provide answers to the questions that follow. Be specific and whenever possible provide examples of the behaviors you reference.**

When you have finished, **place your answers to the following questions in an envelope labeled feedback for _____ and return it to** (<u>designate a person to collect</u>) by (<u>date</u>). They will give me all the envelopes together. **Your feedback will be anonymous and confidential.**

Thank you for making time to provide thoughtful feedback. I value your input. I will share with everyone what I have learned from your feedback.

Please share what you value most about my leadership. What are my greatest strengths? Please provide specific examples.

What behaviors do I need to change?

Based on the needs of the organization what are the areas I need to grow as a leader?

What other feedback can you provide that will help me to become a more effective leader?

Leadership Changes Assessment

As organizations grow, leaders successfully make four major shifts in how they focus their energy and provide leadership to the organization. Place an x where you think you are. Ask staff and board members to assess you as well.

1. From doing to orchestrating.

1	2	3	4	5

Very hands on, solves all problems	Establishes systems and seeks input	Orchestrates work and effectively delegates

2. From directing to teaching and developing others. As the organization grows, leaders spend less time solving problems and overseeing day-to-day operations. They spend more time teaching and developing staff members to work more independently. As the organization develops a clear mission-driven strategy, leaders work with staff members to provide services and make decisions consistent with the organization's mission strategy.

1	2	3	4	5

Directing	Teaching and building trust	Developing capacity of staff to lead

3. From filling funding gaps to building and executing a long-term sustainable resource development strategy.

1	2	3	4	5

Working to meet payroll and reliable cash flow	Building relationships and commitment to mission	Long-term partnership with investors to achieve mission

4. **From focusing on the here and now to developing and sharing a vision and strategy for the future.** As the organization begins to operate effectively, leaders spend more time facilitating the development of a long-term vision for the organization and a strategy for achieving greater impact and reach.

1	2	3	4	5
Short-term goals		Building strategy		Vision, strategy, and operating plan drives work

The Road Ahead

Sample Business Acumen Interview Questions

National nonprofit leaders identified business acumen as one of the critical skills leaders need to be successful. Business acumen involves integrating numerous hard and soft skills with an understanding of sound management practices and a fanatical belief in mission.

The following questions are designed to help board and professional leaders assess business acumen during the hiring process.

1. Please tell me about a time you used your understanding of different parts of the organization to initiate a new project. What was the project? How did your knowledge of the organization make a difference? What was the outcome?

2. Tell me about a time you successfully used knowledge gained from reading a professional publication to strengthen your organization. What was the knowledge? How did you apply it to your organization? What difference did it make?

3. Tell me about the process you use to establish an annual operating plan and the steps you take to execute the plan.

4. What financial information do you look at regularly and how do you use that information? Tell me about a time when the financial information you review alerted you to a problem? What steps did you take to resolve the problem? What was the result?

5. Have you ever exceeded your budget? What was the cause and what steps did you take to address? What have you learned from this experience?

6. How have you used human resource systems to support the organizations goals?

7. Can you give us an example of how you established a goal and vision for a new initiative? Tell us about the goal, how you established a plan, how you executed the plan and what the results were.

References

Adams, Tom, and Jeanne Bell. "Leading for Mission Results: Connecting Leadership Beliefs with Predictable Changes." *Nonprofit Quarterly* (January 23, 2017). https://nonprofitquarterly.org/leading-mission-results-connecting-leadership-beliefs-predictable-changes/.

Alliance for Strong Families and Communities. "A National Imperative: Joining Forces to Strengthen Human Services in America" (2020). https://www.alliance1.org/web/community/national-imperative-joining-forces-strengthen-human-services-america.aspx.

Barr, Kate, and Jeanne Bell. "An Executive Director's Guide to Financial Leadership." *Nonprofit Quarterly* (January 10, 2019). https://nonprofitquarterly.org/executive-directors-guide-financial-leadership-2/.

Bennis, Warren G., and Patricia Ward Biederman. *Organizing Genius: The Secrets of Creative Collaboration* (New York: Basic Books, 1997).

Bennis, Warren, and Noel Tichy. *Judgement: How Winning Leaders Make Great Calls* (New York: Penguin Group, 2007).

Berlan, David. "Understanding Nonprofit Missions as Dynamic and Interpretative Conceptions." *Nonprofit Management & Leadership* 28, no. 3 (Spring 2018): 413–422.

BoardSource. "Leading with Intent: National Index of Nonprofit Board Practices" (2017). https://leadingwithintent.org/wp-content/uploads/2017/11/LWI-2017.pdf?hsCtaTracking=8736f801–1e14–427b-adf0–38485b149ac0%7C82ace287-b110–4d8f-9651–2b2c06a43c05.

Boys & Girls Clubs of America (BGCA). "Clubs Measure Up: A Guide to Measurement Strategies" (2006).

Brown, Brené. "*The Power of Vulnerability*." TED Talk (2012).

Building Movement Project. "Trading Glass Ceilings for Glass Cliffs: A Race to Lead Report on Nonprofit Executives of Color" (2022). https://buildingmovement.org/wp-content/uploads/2022/02/Race-to-Lead-ED-CEO-Report-2.8.22.pdf.

Burns, James M. *Transforming Leadership* (New York: Grove Press, 2003).

Carver, John. *Boards That Make a Difference* (San Francisco: Jossey-Bass, 2006).

Cermak, Jenny, and Monica McGurk. "Putting a Value on Training." *McKinsey Quarterly* (July 2010).

Collins, Jim. *Good to Great* (New York: Harper Business, 2001).

Collins, Jim. *Good to Great and the Social Sector: Monograph to Accompany Good to Great* (New York: Harper Business, 2005).

Doerr, John. *Measure What Matters: How Google, Bono and the Gates Foundation Rock the World with OKRs* (New York: Portfolio/Penguin, 2018).

Drucker, Peter F. *Managing the Non-Profit Organization* (New York: Harper Business, 1990).

Dweck, Carol. *Mindset: The New Psychology of Success* (New York: Random House, 2006).

Forbes Nonprofit Council. "Eight Ways Your Nonprofit Can Address and Survive the Labor Shortage" (2019).

Frey, William H. "New 2020 Census Results Show Increased Diversity Countering Decade-Long Declines in America's White and Youth Populations." Brookings Institution. (2021). https://www.brookings.edu/research/new-2020-census-results-show-increased-diversity-countering-decade-long-declines-in-americas-white-and-youth-populations/.

Garry, Joan. *Joan Garry's Guide to Nonprofit Leadership* (Hoboken, NJ: John Wiley and Sons, 2017).

Gladwell, Malcom. *David and Goliath* (Boston: Little, Brown and Company, 2015).

Goldsmith, Marshall. *What Got You Here Won't Get You There* (New York: Hyperion, 2007).

Goldstein, Dana. "Why You Can't Find Child Care." *New York Times* (October 2022).

Goulston, Mark, and Patricia Romboletti. "Top Five Ways to Mess up Hiring the Right CEO." BoardSource. https://boardsource.org/resources/top-five-ways-mess-hiring-right-ceo/.

Grace, Kay Sprinkle. *Beyond Fundraising: New Strategies for Nonprofits* (Hoboken, NJ: John Wiley and Sons, 2005).

Grant, Adam. *Think Again* (New York: Penguin Random House, 2021).

Greszler, Rachel. "An Unprecedented Labor Shortage." Heritage Foundation (2022).

Inc. "Nonprofit Organizations, and Human Resource Management." https://www.inc.com/encyclopedia/nonprofit-organizations-and-human-resources-management.html.

Jennings, Jason. *Think Big Act Small* (New York: Portfolio/Penguin, 2012).

Hansen-Turton, Tine, Richard J. Cohen, and Nicholas D. Torres. *Partnerships for Health and Human Service Nonprofits: From Collaborations to Mergers* (New York: Springer Publishing Company, 2015).

Kania, John, and Mark Kramer. "Collective Impact." *Stanford Social Innovation Review* (Winter 2011).

Kania, John, Junious Williams, Paul Schmitz, Sheri Brady, Mark Kramer, and Jennifer Splansky Juster. "Centering Equity in Collective Impact." *Stanford Social Innovation Review* (2021).

Lencioni, Patrick. *Four Obsessions of an Extraordinary Executive* (San Francisco: Jossey-Bass, 2000).

MacNamara, Carter. "Guidelines and Framework for Developing a Basic Logic Model. *Management Library* (September 23, 2022). https://managementhelp.org/freenonprofittraining/diagramming-your-nonprofit.htm.

McChesney, Chris, Sean Covey, and Jim Huling. *The Four Disciplines of Execution* (New York: Simon and Schuster, 2012).

Mintzberg, Henry. "The Rise and Fall of Strategic Planning." *Harvard Business Review* (1994).

Moore, Mark. "Managing for Value: Organizational Strategy in For-Profit, Nonprofit and Governmental Organizations." *Nonprofit and Voluntary Sector Quarterly* 29, no. 1 (2000).

Morino, Mario. *Leap of Reason: Managing to Outcomes in an Era of Scarcity* (Washington, DC: Venture Philanthropy Partners, 2011).

National Council of Nonprofits. "Nonprofit Audit Guide." https://www.councilof nonprofits.org/nonprofit-audit-guide.

National Council of Nonprofits. "The Scope and Impact of Nonprofit Workforce Shortages (2021)." (2021). https://bit.ly/3x5OWZs.

Pandy, Sheela, Mirae Ki, and Sanja K. Pandey. "Do Mission Statements Matter for Nonprofit Performance?" *Nonprofit Management & Leadership* 27, no. 3 (Spring 2017): 389–410.

Permuy, Glenn. "Toughest Job in America." *Connections Magazine* (1998).

Poister, Theodore H., Maria P. Aristigueta, and Jeremy L. Hall. *Measuring Performance in Public and Nonprofit Organizations: An Integrated Approach* (San Francisco: Jossey-Bass, 2015).

Pynes, Joan E. *Human Resources Management for Public and Nonprofit Organizations* (San Francisco: Jossey-Bass, 2013).

Ramalingam, Ben, David Nabarro, Arkebe Oqubay, Dame Ruth Carnell, and Leni Wild. "5 Principles to Guide Adaptive Leaders" *Harvard Business Review* (2020).

Seyhan, Osman. "A Primer for Transformational Leadership in Nonprofit Sector." *Academia* (2013).

Tebbe, Don. *Chief Executive Transitions: How to Hire and Support a Nonprofit CEO* (Washington, DC: BoardSource, 2019).

Tichy, Noel, and Nancy Cardwell. *The Cycle of Leadership* (New York: Harper Business, 2002).

"Trends for Nonprofit Leaders to Watch in 2022." *Forbes Magazine* (2022).

Urban Institute. "*The Nonprofit Sector in Brief*" (June 2020). https://nccs.urban.org/publication/nonprofit-sector-brief-2019.

U.S. Chamber of Commerce. "Understanding America's Labor Shortage" (2022). https://www.uschamber.com/workforce/understanding-americas-labor-shortage.

Wings for Kids. (n.d.a). "Four Year Randomized Control Study Executive Summary" https://www.wingsforkids.org/sel/approach/program-evidence/.

Wings for Kids. (n.d.b). "Social Emotional Learning: Equipping Kids with Skills for Success." https://www.wingsforkids.org/sel/social-emotional-learning/.

Wings for Kids. (n.d.c). "Social Emotional Learning: The New Smart." https://www.wingsforkids.org/sel/.

Wings for Kids. (n.d.d). "Social Emotional Learning: Our Approach to Social Emotional Learning." https://www.wingsforkids.org/sel/approach/.

Wings for Kids. (n.d.e.). Social Emotional Learning: Research and Evidence. https://www.wingsforkids.org/sel/approach/program-evidence/.

About the Author

Ed Mishrell believes the most successful nonprofit organizations are blessed with extraordinary leadership. Ed started his career as a probation officer. He then went to graduate school to learn more about what made organizations successful. He has held many positions in the nonprofit sector including childcare director, senior citizen center director, teen program director, youth employment director, and community center director. In 1986 he joined the national office of Boys & Girls Clubs of America (BGCA), where he led the development of numerous strategic initiatives including outcome measurement, executive leadership development, deepening impact, ensuring public trust, and creating national program initiatives supporting academic success and technology. He led the creation of the Spillett Leadership University and the Advance Leadership Program for executive development. The impact of the Advance Leadership Program was documented in an article published in *McKinsey Quarterly* entitled "Putting a Value on Training" (Cermak and McGurk, 2010).

Ed served as the chief strategy officer for BGCA from 2010 to 2019. He worked closely with local club board and professional leaders and BGCA staff and national board members to lead the development and deployment of BGCA's strategic and operating plans. Ed is a talented speaker and presenter. He has led hundreds of leadership training programs and continues to serve as a faculty member for BGCA's Advanced Leadership Program. He has spoken at numerous regional and national conferences for Boys & Girls Clubs, other nonprofit organizations, and has even made a presentation on workforce development at the United Nations.

When he retired from BGCA Ed taught a graduate course at the Andrew Young School of Public Policy at Georgia State University. While searching for material about leadership in nonprofits for his students, Ed began interviewing successful nonprofit leaders to capture what made them successful. These interviews became the foundation for 5 *Truths for Transformational Leaders*.

Ed has authored numerous articles and program resources used by more than 50,000 professional staff and board members at Boys & Girls Clubs. This includes booklets and resources to guide hiring practices, ethics, financial management, ensuring accurate data, measuring outcomes, supervision, and leadership development. Ed is the recipient of numerous awards including the Thomas G. Garth Character and Courage Award, the highest honor a BGCA leader can receive.

Ed holds a bachelor of science degree from Alfred University, a Master of education from Elmira College, and a master of social work administration from Temple University.

Index